The
Cricke

THE ARMADA
CRICKET QUIZ BOOK

by Gordon Jeffery

Armada

On the cover:
Front (from left to right): Tony Greig, W. G. Grace, Jeff
Thomson, Don Bradman, W. Voce, John Snow, Alan Knott,
W. A. Brown.
Back: Colin Cowdrey, Basil D'Oliveira, Charlie Griffiths,
Richard Hutton, Fred Trueman, D. R. Jardine.

The Armada Cricket Quiz Book
was first published in 1975
by Wm. Collins Sons & Co. Ltd.,
14 St. James's Place, London SW1A 1PF

© Gordon Jeffery 1975

Printed in Great Britain by
Love & Malcomson Ltd., Brighton Road,
Redhill, Surrey.

1. COUNTY BADGES – 1

Below are the badges of two of the seventeen counties who compete in the County Championship each season. (The badges of the remaining fifteen counties, in sets of three, are illustrated in Puzzles 11, 18, 33, 43 and 54.)

Can you fill in (a) the name of the county, (b) the county colours, and (c) a description of the badge?

A

B

2. SOME CRICKET TERMS

1. In the United Kingdom an 'over' consists of six consecutive fair deliveries bowled from the same wicket. What is a 'maiden over'?

2. What is a 'wicket maiden'?

3. The cricket score of each side is reckoned by runs. Runs are scored by the batsmen and by – who else?

4. What is a 'duck'?

5. What is the 'on' side of a cricket pitch?

6. What is the 'off' side of a cricket pitch?

7. What is a 'ton'?

8. If the breakdown of the 'extras' recorded on a scorecard is shown as 2B, 4LB, 2W, 1NB, what do the letters stand for?

9. What is a 'pair of spectacles'?

10. Who is a 'nightwatchman'?

3. TAKING GUARD – AN EASY START

1. What do the initials M.C.C. stand for in (a) England (b) Australia?

2. Can you name the famous English Test batsman who has the same initials?

3. How many days are allowed for play in a County Championship match?

4. How many days are normally allowed for play in Test matches?

5. How many overs can each side bat, unless dismissed, in Benson and Hedges Cup matches?

6. How many in John Player League matches?

7. How many in Gillette Cup matches?

8. From 1974, the length of each side's first innings in County Championship matches was limited by rule. What was the maximum number of overs that could be faced by (a) the side batting first and (b) their opponents?

9. Who was England's captain in the 1974 Test matches played against the West Indies, India and Pakistan?

10. And who was the captain in the 1973 Test matches played in England against the West Indies?

4. A LOOK AROUND THE FIELD –
NOT SO EASY!

In the three Test matches played against India in 1974 –

1. In the first Test who scored a century for England in their first innings?

2. Who followed with a century when the Indians batted in their first innings?

3. In England's second innings the captain declared at 213 for 3. An English batsman was then 100 not out. Can you name him?

4. England won the match when the Indians were dismissed for 182 in their second innings. The most successful bowler took 4 for 20. Who was he?

5. Who was brought into the side as opener for the Second Test in preference to Geoff Boycott?

6. In England's only innings in the Second Test, three batsmen made centuries. Who were they? To help remind you – their actual scores were 188, 118 (a maiden Test century) and 106.

7. India scored 302 in their first innings but had to follow-on and were scuttled out for 42. Main damage was done by two English bowlers who took 5 for 21 and 4 for 19. Which two bowlers respectively?

8. On which grounds were the (a) First (b) Second and (c) Third Tests played against India?

9. A feature of England's batting in the Third Test was the score of 214 runs made by a player appearing in only his second Test match. Can you name him?

10. A sadder feature in the Indian second innings was the dismissal of A. V. Mankad. This is recorded correctly as 'hit wicket bowled Old' but what were the unusual circumstances?

5. FIND THE BATSMEN

The names of two great cricketers of to-day are coded in this diagram. Both have played for their country in Test matches and both headed the batting averages for their English counties in 1974. Can you name them? What countries and what counties do they play for?

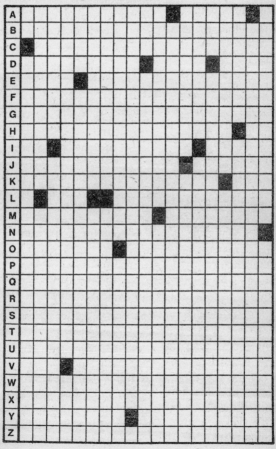

6. THOSE INITIALS . . .

The line-ups of football teams usually show only the surnames of the players, but the batting order of cricket teams more often give the players' initials in addition to their surnames. Many years ago you could pick out the amateur from the professional player because the amateur's initials would be printed in front of his surname.

Here is a selection of some famous players of the past. With the clues to help you (and maybe also the help of your father or even your grandfather!) can you complete their names?

1. B. J. T. B ———————   Regarded as being the inventor of the 'googly'

2. L. E. G. A ———   Wicket-keeper and batsman for Kent and England

3. P. G. H. F —————   Spectacled Surrey allrounder. A mighty hitter – and a useful goalkeeper for, amongst others, the Corinthians

4. D. V. P. W —————   He took over 2,000 wickets for Kent from 1932 to 1957

5. C. W. L. P —————   Slow left-arm bowler who played for Gloucestershire from 1905 to 1935 and took over 100 wickets in each of his last 16 seasons

6. A. P. F. C ——————   Captain of Kent and England.

Probably the best-remembered of all initials were those of the Essex and England captain immediately before and after the First World War. His name was J. W. H. T. Douglas.. Do you know the phrase that was made using the initial letters J.W.H.T.D.?

7. FACING THE BOWLING

1. Ten of the West Indian team who played against India at Bangalore in the first Test match of their 1974-75 tour are on the playing staff of British counties. Who was the odd man out?

2. Who was the West Indian captain in that match and throughout the tour?

3. For which country did a contractor and an engineer play Test cricket?

4. Julian Shackleton (Gloucestershire) and Bob Herman (Hampshire – he previously played for Middlesex) are the sons of two former Hampshire bowlers. Which, if either or both of them, was born in Hampshire?

5. Who was the first player to score a six off every ball of a six-balls over in a first-class cricket match?

6. The 1974 season opened at Lord's with a match between the County Champions and MCC. Who, on the first day, opened the innings and had scored 189 out of a total of 249 for six before he was dismissed? (he made his runs in $3\frac{1}{2}$ hours and hit two sixes and 32 fours.)

7. On the same day, playing for D. H. Robins XI at Eastbourne against the Indian tourists, a Warwickshire batsman scored his second century of the match. Who was he?

8. In a 1974 County Championship match Notts were hustled out for 94 runs. A. L. 'Rocker' Robinson (5 for 27) and Dennis Schofield (5 for 42) took the Notts wickets. For which county were they playing?

9. In one of his country's pre-Test matches in 1974, a Pakistani bowler had a career-best analysis of 10.4 overs, 3 maidens, 27 runs and 8 wickets. Can you name him?

10. On the same day a Leicestershire batsman, also well-known as a footballer, had a remarkable innings, scoring 140 out of his side's total of 216 all out. He was . . . ?

8. SIX SCRAMBLED PLAYERS

This scramble of letters, with each letter used only once, spells the names of six cricketers who played for England during the 1974 Test matches. The number of dots below is the same as the number of letters to each player's surname – only three dots for one of the names may help you get off to a flying start!

1. - - - - -   4. - - - - - -

2. - - - - -   5. - - - - - -

3. - - -   6. - - - - -

9. GREAT NAMES IN CRICKET – I

He was born on 18th July, 1848, at Downend, Bristol; the son of a doctor, which he was to become himself in the course of time. Father – and mother – were also cricket lovers and from an early age our player and his brothers were coached in the game.

Christened William Gilbert, but to be generally known in the world of cricket by his initials 'W.G.', our mystery player was an eager pupil and played his first match for West Gloucestershire just one day after his ninth birthday. He scored 3 not out – but before he finally set his bat aside it has been estimated that in all matches he scored about 80,000 runs.

He made his first appearance in 'big' cricket in 1864 – the year in which what can be accepted as a regular series for the County Championship began. It was also the year in which 'overhand bowling' was authorised and W.G.'s prowess as a bowler should not be forgotten.

It was, however, as a batsman that he first attracted national attention. He was two days short of his sixteenth birthday when he played for the South Wales Club against the Gentlemen of Sussex. He scored 170 and 56 not out.

The County Championship had only just begun and 16 years were to pass before the first Test match was played in England. Club cricket with occasional county and other big matches was the scene in the 1860's. The extent of the game had broadened considerably by the time. W.G played his last first-class match in 1908 (he died in 1915) but he, more than any other player, had dominated the scene for much of that time.

The record books are studded with his performances. In 1871, for instance, he was the first batsman to exceed 2,000 runs in first-class cricket in a season. It was a further 22 years before any other batsman achieved that, but W.G. did it six times – and took wickets as a bowler. In 1873 he scored 2,139 runs and took 106 wickets (the first ever 'double' of 1,000 runs and 100 wickets in a season). In 1876 he scored 2,622 runs and took 129 wickets.

At that time, perhaps even more than now, professional cricketers depended upon benefit matches to bring in money against the time of their retirement from the game. The appearance of 'W.G.' (and a big score) was valuable, and the professionals concerned were not disappointed by his scores in three benefit matches in 1871 – 189 not out, 268, and 217.

In eight days in August 1876, W.G. scored 344 runs for M.C.C. playing against Kent at Canterbury. This was the first score of over 300 runs in first-class cricket but, within those eight days, he went on to score 177 for his county, Gloucestershire, against Nottinghamshire, and 318 not out for Gloucestershire against Yorkshire.

In 1880 the first Test Match was played in England – at the Oval – between England and Australia. W.G. was in the England team, together with his brothers, E. M. and G. F. (their only Test appearances; W.G. appeared in 22). England won the match by five wickets with W.G. scoring 152 in England's first innings of 420.

In 1895 another record was established by W.G. when he became the first batsman to score 1,000 runs in May (the feat was not repeated until Wally Hammond did it in 1927), and in the same year 'W.G.' scored his 100th century. When he finally retired, his career record in first-class matches was the astonishing one of 54,896 runs, 2,876 wickets and 871 catches.

Can you supply the surname to those famous initials – W.G.?

10. EARLY DAYS OF CRICKET

Here are the names of four of the early patrons and/or players who, in the first half of the 18th century, were prominent in arranging cricket matches in their counties. Each has been described as the 'father of cricket' in his particular county. But in the table below, the names and counties have been mixed up. Can you match them up correctly?

1. (a) Edwin Stead (originally Stede)   – Hampshire
   (b) Sir William Gage   – Kent
   (c) Frederic, Prince of Wales (son of
       King George II)   – Sussex
   (d) Charles Powlett   – Surrey

2. Which cricketer was known as 'The Lion of Kent'?

3. Under which name was Nicholas Wanostrocht known as a cricketer? The single name, one of only five letters, (famous much later on film as the name of a cat!), was written on the bat he used.

4. What was the first name of the famous bowler 'Lumpy' Stevens?

11. COUNTY BADGES – 2

Here are three more badges to identify. Can you in each case name (a) the county, and (b) the county colours, and (c) describe the badge?

A

B

C

12. THE COUNTY CHAMPIONSHIP

The County Championship dates from 1864. Qualification rules, including the rule that no player should play for more than one county during the same season, were first agreed in July 1873, at which time nine counties were considered first-class. One of these was Derbyshire, who dropped out in 1887 and re-appeared in 1895. Hampshire, not amongst the original nine, were only considered first-class between 1875–78 and 1880–85, and were also finally admitted in 1895. There are now seventeen counties competing each season for the Championship.

1. How many of the original nine counties, including Derbyshire, can you name?

2. In addition to Hampshire and Derbyshire, three other counties were admitted for the first time in 1895. Which ones?

3. Somerset had been admitted in 1891, and two more were admitted before the outbreak of the First World War (bringing the total to 16 in the competition). Which county was admitted in (a) 1899 and (b) 1905.

4. Which was the seventeenth county admitted – in 1921?

5. One of the nine competing counties in 1873 has yet to win the Championship. Which one?

6. Two players – one for Yorkshire and one for Kent – made more than 700 appearances in County Championship matches. Can you name them?

13. BEST WITH BAT AND BALL – 1

In the 1974 County Championship matches who:

1. Headed the batting averages for Kent? He scored 1,035 runs in 30 completed innings.

2. Took the most wickets for Leicestershire – 57 of them?

3. Had the best bowling analysis for Essex? He took 68 wickets with an average of 18.05.

4. Headed the battering averages for Middlesex with 1,292 runs in 29 completed innings?

5. Had the best bowling analysis for Hampshire? He took 111 wickets with an average of 13.45.

6. Who scored the most runs for Somerset – 1,154 of them?

7. Headed the bowling averages for Derbyshire? He took 34 wickets with an average of 18.74.

8. Scored the most runs for Surrey – 907 of them?

9. Headed Worcestershire's batting averages with 1,098 runs in 20 completed innings?

10. Took the most wickets for Nottinghamshire – 73 of them?

14. FIELDING – 1

Here is an illustration of a typical field placing for a fast or medium pace right-handed bowler bowling out-swingers in a County Championship match. Can you indicate alongside each of the fielders the name given to their fielding position? Wicket-keeper, mid-on, cover, etc.

(See also Puzzles 24, 41 and 51)

15. TEST APPEARANCES

1. How many Test appearances did Tom Graveney make for England?
   - (a) Up to 25
   - (b) Between 26 and 50
   - (c) Between 51 and 75
   - (d) Over 75

2. Can you place the following players in order of the number of appearances each made for England? First place, of course, to the player who made the most appearances.
   (a) Jack Hobbs (b) Len Hutton (c) Peter May (d) Ken Barrington

   1st ....
   2nd ....
   3rd ....
   4th ....

3. How many Test appearances did Don Bradman make for Australia?
   - (a) Up to 25
   - (b) Between 26 and 50
   - (c) Between 51 and 75
   - (d) Over 75

4. How many appearances has Barry Richards made in officially recognised Test matches for South Africa?

5. Place the following players in order of the number of appearances they made for Australia in Test matches.
   (a) Keith Miller (b) Richie Benaud (c) Norman O'Neill (d) Ray Lindwall

   1st ....
   2nd ....
   3rd ....
   4th ....

6. Who holds the record for the most Test appearances for the West Indies?

7. Place in order of their appearance for the West Indies in Test matches the three famous Ws.
(a) Clyde Walcott (b) Everton Weekes (c) Frank Worrell

   1st   ....
   2nd   ....
   3rd   ..:.............................

8. Back to England, and do you know how many Test appearances C. P. Mead made for England? (He made more runs in County championship matches than any other player.)
   (a) Up to 25
   (b) Between 26 and 50
   (c) Between 51 and 75
   (d) Over 75

9. Four English pace bowlers (a) Harold Larwood (b) Fred Trueman (c) Frank Tyson (d) Bill Bowes. Can you place them in the order of their appearances in Test matches for England?
   1st   ....
   2nd   ....
   3rd   ....
   4th   ....

10. How many times did E. R. 'Ted' Dexter of Sussex play for England in Test matches?
   (a) Up to 25
   (b) Between 26 and 50
   (c) Between 51 and 75
   (d) Over 75

16. UP FOR THE CUP!

That familiar football cry is now to be heard on English cricket grounds. The *two* Cups that have captured the interest of cricket fans (and television viewers) are the limited-over Gillette and Benson & Hedges competitions. What do you remember of the 1974 Finals for these two competitions?

1. The Benson & Hedges Final was contested between Leicestershire and Surrey. Who won and by what margin?

2. Who, in the Benson & Hedges Cup Final, captained (a) Surrey and (b) Leicestershire?

3. Who won the Gillette Cup Final played between Kent and Lancashire?

4. Who kept wicket in the Gillette Cup Final for (a) Kent and (b) Lancashire?

5. In Surrey's Benson & Hedges innings, the Leicestershire wicket-keeper claimed four victims – all of them caught. Can you name the keeper?

6. Who was the bowler who did the hat-trick in the Benson & Hedges Final?

7. He was only the second bowler in the three years since this competition started to do the hat-trick. Who was the first bowler to do so? (He was playing for the same county.)

8. The same rule denied Surrey, in the Benson and Hedges Final, and Kent, in the Gillette Final, of the services of one of their leading players. What was the ruling? And who were the two players concerned?

9. Who was the top scorer in the Gillette Final and how many runs did he score?

10. Who was awarded the 'Man of the Match' bonus in (a) the Benson and Hedges and (b) the Gillette Finals?

17. GREAT NAMES IN CRICKET – 2

In 1908, sixty years after W.G. was born (see Puzzle No. 9), in fact in the year he played first-class cricket for the last time, a boy was born at Cootamundra, New South Wales, Australia, who grew up to become the greatest run-scoring cricketer the world has ever seen.

He was educated at Bowral Intermediate High School and made his first appearance for New South Wales in 1927. It was first first-class match and he played against South Australia (a state for whom he was to play from 1935 until his retirement in 1949). Our player scored 118 runs and went on for the rest of his career to average a century on every third visit to the wicket.

His story is the story of cricketing records – too many of them to list here. In his second season for New South Wales he set up the record for runs in an Australian season – 1,690 runs in 24 innings. He was not out six times and his batting average was thus 93.88. The number of first-class matches played in Australia was much fewer than in England but our player still contrived to score over 1,000 runs in 12 Australian seasons. In each of his four seasons in England with the Australian touring party he topped 2,000 runs – and each time headed the batting averages for first-class matches played that season in England.

At home in Australia in the 1929–30 season he scored 452 not out for New South Wales against Queensland – a record that stood for nearly 30 years. The following summer, at the age of 21, he made his first visit to England. He took strike for the first time on 30th April at Worcester, where traditionally the Australians played their first match. At the close of play he had scored 75 not out. The next day he continued to complete a 'first appearance in England' innings of 236, and by the end of May he had scored 1,000 runs for an average of 143. Only four batsmen before him had scored 1,000 runs in England before the end of May – and he had done so on his first appearance.

By the end of the 1930 season he had scored 2,960 runs with an average of 98.66. His highest score was 334 – and that score was made in the.Third Test Match at Leeds. In the course of that historic innings he had reached 200 runs in 214 minutes, and in the course of a single day he scored 309 runs!

In 1938, when he again scored over 1,000 runs by the end of May, his batting average after 26 innings (five times not out) in England was 115.66 – the first time that a season's average had topped the century mark.

In 1948, with the war years intervening and our player approaching his fortieth birthday it seemed that the flow of runs must have slowed, but he again topped the averages with 2,428 runs and an average of 89.92. Yet there was one 'failure'. On his last Test appearance at the Oval in 1948 he was out for a duck. It left him with a Test career batting record of :

Tests	Innings	Not Out	Runs	Highest Score	100's	Average
52	80	10	6,996	334	29	99.94

Seventy completed innings so if he had scored just four runs and not nought in his last innings, his Test career average would have been exactly 100. But in fact his Test average of 99.94 was higher than his average for all first-class matches – which was 95.14 with a total of 28,067 runs, including 117 centuries made out of 338 innings.

He was knighted in 1949 and after his retirement served as an Australian Test selector. Cricket will probably never again see a batsman to equal the records of ....
Can you name him?

Three more county badges. Can you again (a) name the county, (b) name the county colours, and (c) give a description of the badge?

A

B

C

19. SOME FAMOUS BATSMEN

In the following list of 15 Test cricketers, four played for England, four for Australia, two for the West Indies, two for South Africa, and one each for India, New Zealand and Pakistan. Can you complete the table showing the country for which each played and then tick the period in which they appeared in Test matches. Some, of course, played in more than one of the periods.

	Country	A 1914 & before	B 1919-1939	C 1946-66	D 1967 onwards
1. Geoff Boycott	....	...	...	...	...
2. Don Bradman	....	...	...	...	...
3. Martin Donnelly	....	...	...	...	...
4. George Headley Senr.	....	...	...	...	...
5. Jack Hobbs	....	...	...	...	...
6. Len Hutton	....	...	...	...	...
7. Bill Lawry	....	...	...	...	...
8. Peter May	....	...	...	...	...
9. Vijay Merchant	....	...	...	...	...
10. Hanif Mohammad	....	...	...	...	...
11. Dudley Nourse Jnr.	....	...	...	...	...
12. Bill Ponsford	....	...	...	...	...
13. Gary Sobers	....	...	...	...	...
14. Herbert Taylor	....	...	...	...	...
15. Vic Trumper	....	...	...	...	...

20. SOME CORNER OF A FOREIGN FIELD

Where would an M.C.C. touring team be playing cricket if they were on the following grounds?

1. Sabina Park

2. Railway Stadium

3. Wanderers Ground

4. Eden Park

5. Eden Gardens

6. Woolloongabba

7. Queen's Park Oval

8. Lancaster Park

9. Newlands

10. Kensington Oval

21. THEY MAKE CRICKET

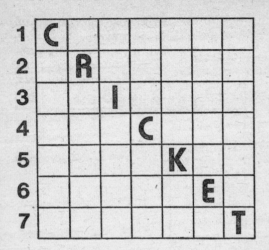

1. Promising young Yorkshire all-rounder who made his County debut in 1970.
2. Gloucestershire's exciting quick-scoring batsman and fast bowler.
3. Australian all-rounder who served Lancashire well in the fifties – when he also played in goal for Bury and Bolton Wanderers.
4. Yorkshire captain and opener. Batting hero of England's 1974 victory over the West Indies.
5. A Northamptonshire stalwart for many seasons. Made his county debut in 1934 and was appointed captain twenty years later. Scored over 2,000 runs in the 1952 season.
6. M.C.C. – the cricketer not the club! Debut for Kent in 1950 and still going strong!
7. Hampshire's popular captain and useful middle-order batsman.

22. EIGHT AUSSIES

Complete the squares by identifying the Australian players from the clues given below. Then fill in the strip at the bottom of the page by working out the grid references. That will give you the prize at stake when England and Australia play against each other. (If, of course, you guess the prize first, that will help you with the main puzzle.)

	1	2	3	4	5	6	7	8
A								
B								
C								
D								
E								
F								
G								
H								

A. The initials before his surname are K.D. but he is known generally as Doug.
B. Greg or Ian?
C. Sounds like a flower but looks fierce to batsmen
D. Ashley with a wooden hammer?
E. Leading wicket-taker in the 1974-75 Test series
F. Experienced batsman who played in all the Test matches in England in 1964 and 1968
G. No. 3 seam bowler
H. But he does not play football for Manchester City!

A4	B2	C6		D2	E5	F7	G5	H4

23. PLAYERS IN DISGUISE

The familiar first name and the surname of well-known cricketers are hidden in the following anagrams – and the numbers of letters in their names are shown.

1. DICK HIKER MEN   ---- ---------

2. RUDE FEN TRAM   ---- -------

3. TRAINS BUSY PEER   ----- ----------

4. BOOM BLOWER   --- --------

5. LIE VERY CLAD   ----- ------

6. BBC TOMATO   --- ------

7. BESS OR GRAY   ---- ------

8. TART MIGHT CROW   --- -----------

9. GOLF AND FORE   ----- ------

10. DON FOR FARMING   ------ -------

24. FIELDING – 2

Here is another illustration of a typical field placing, but in this case the fast or medium pace right-handed bowler is bowling in-swingers in a County Championship match. Can you mark in the names of the fielding positions occupied? And can you explain the differences between this field placing and that for Puzzle 14?

25. BEST WITH BAT AND BALL – 2

In the 1974 County Championship matches, who:

1. Headed the bowling averages for Glamorgan with 63 wickets and an average of 23.22?

2. Headed Gloucestershire's batting averages – 1,196 runs and 28 finished innings?

3. Took the most wickets for Sussex – 70 of them?

4. Scored the most runs for Northamptonshire – 1,845 of them?

5. Scored the most runs for Warwickshire – 1,420 of them?

6. Headed the batting averages for Lancashire with 1,403 runs and 22 finished innings?

7. Headed the batting averages for Hampshire? He scored 1,059 runs and had 19 finished innings.

8. Had the best bowling analysis for Middlesex? He took 21 wickets and had an average of 21.47.

9. Headed the batting averages for Essex – 32 completed innings and 1,062 runs?

10. With an average of 17.18 and a bag of 33 wickets, headed Yorkshire's bowling averages?

26. ODD MAN OUT

In each of the following sets of five cricketers, four of them have one thing in common that the fifth has not. Can you name the odd man out in each case?

1. Keith Boyce, Roy Fredericks, Farokh Engineer, Gordon Greenidge, John Shepherd

2. Brian Bolus, Trevor Jesty, Ray East, Peter Sainsbury, Derek Underwood

3. Peter Lever, Geoff Arnold, Fred Titmus, John Snow, Chris Old

4. John Murray, Barry Wood, Alan Knott, Bob Stephenson, Bob Taylor

5. Clive Radley, Tony Lewis, Roger Knight, Richard Gilliat, Colin Cowdrey

6. Majid Khan, Zaheer Abbas, Asif Iqbal, Intikhab Alam, Bishen Bedi

7. Tony Greig, Basil D'Oliveira, Barry Richards, Brian Davison, Mike Procter

8. Ian Buxton, Arthur Milton, Roger Prideaux, Chris Balderstone, Ted Hemsley

9. David Lloyd, Keith Fletcher, Brian Luckhurst, Geoff Boycott, John Edrich

10. Dennis Amiss, Bob Woolmer, Colin Cowdrey, Robin Jackman, John Jameson

27. GREAT NAMES IN CRICKET – 3

Many famous cricketers have had their first experience of first-class cricket playing for Cambridge University. One of the greatest of all English batsman was in fact born there on 16th December, 1882. In time he began playing cricket for Cambridgeshire but aiming to succeed beyond the opportunities offered by a 'Minor County', he offered his services to the neighbouring, and first-class county club, Essex.

Essex turned him down, but soon afterwards a fellow-townsman, Tom Hayward (born at Cambridge eleven years before our player and from 1893 the regular opening batsman for Surrey), introduced our player to the Surrey club and personally recommended him. Surrey gave him a trial and for the next two years he played for the Surrey Club and Ground – in effect the Surrey Second XI.

In 1905 he was given his chance, as the opener with Hayward, and played his first County match for Surrey. Quite by chance it was against Essex, the county that had rejected him. In that match he scored an innings of 155 runs! And, as if to rub salt into Essex's wounds, the only other century he scored in his debut season was also against Essex.

Over the next thirty years it was not only Essex who were to suffer from the fine batting of this player who was able to make big scores against any type of bowling and on any sort of wicket. Batting that brought him, from 1905 to 1934, a total of 61,237 runs with an average of 50.65 and included 197 centuries.

For most of his playing career with Surrey, and also for England in Test matches, he was associated with regular opening partners with whom he made many century stands. With Surrey, he shared in 40 century stands with Tom Hayward, including four in a single week in 1907 and one massive stand of 352 against Warwickshire at the Oval in

1909. After Hayward's retirement, our player's opening partner for Surrey was Andrew Sandham and together they put together 63 opening stands of a century or more. (In County partnerships only the famous Yorkshire pair of Holmes and Sutcliffe made more century stands.)

Herbert Sutcliffe was our player's most frequent partner in opening century stands in Test matches – in fifteen of them including three in consecutive innings during England's 1924-25 tour of Australia when they scored 157 and 110 at Sydney followed by 283 at Melbourne.

Our player made his first Test appearance in Australia in 1907 and his last in England against the Australians in 1930 – at the same time as the great Don Bradman was making his first appearances in Test cricket in England. In all, our player played for England in 61 Test matches, batted in 102 innings (seven times being not out), aggregated 5,410 runs with 211 his highest Test match score and an average of 56.94.

He was forty when he made his 100th century – and went on to make 97 more centuries in first-class cricket. Indeed he enjoyed more success, in terms of batting averages, after he was forty than he had before. For instance, he had been second in the season's batting averages in 1913 and 1914, third in 1919 (when first-class cricket was resumed after the First World War), second in 1920, 1922 and 1924 but then first in 1925 (in his 43rd year) and again first in 1926, 1928 and 1929. These accomplishments were the more remarkable because in 1921, due to injury and then a serious illness he only appeared once for Surrey in county championship matches.

He retired in 1935 but may always be remembered at the Oval by the Gate named after him. In 1953 he was knighted in the Coronation Honours List and he died in 1963 – five days after his 81st birthday.

Can you identify him?

28. PIN-POINT THE COUNTIES

Below is a map of England and Wales with the county boundaries, still operative for cricket purposes, indicated. Seventeen of the counties take part in the County Championship. Can you shade them in and name them?

29. RAIN STOPPED PLAY

Rain stopped play! How often those three words have announced the end of hopes of a victory on the field. And how often have they brought, for young cricket fans in particular, the question – what do we do now? Well, here is a cricket game that (with variations that you can make as you wish) has been played indoors on wet days for at least the past fifty years!

It is based upon giving cricket values to the letters of the alphabet like this:

a – 0 runs	i – 0 runs	†p – 3 runs	v – 6 runs
b – bowled	j – 4 runs	q – 6 runs	w – 4 runs
c – caught	k – 4 runs	r – 2 runs	x – 6 runs
d – 2 runs	l – lbw	ro – run out	y – extra run
e – 1 run	m – 4 runs	s – 2 runs	z – 6 runs
f – 3 runs	n – 1 run	st – stumped	
g – 2 runs	no – no ball	t – 4 runs	
*h – 2 runs	o – 2 runs	u – 6 runs	

To produce a more realistic innings, after the fall of the 5th wicket *'h' (hit wicket) and †'p' (played on) are treated as 'bowled'. (Note – when the letters 's' and 't' follow each other, as in the word 'fir*st*' or in the words 'a*s t*he', they lose their individual values and are treated together to represent 'stumped'. Similarly the letters 'r' and 'o' together represent 'run out' and 'n' and 'o' together represent 'no ball'.)

The match is between two sides, of course. You can play it alone or with a friend but either way you toss for which side is going to bat first and write in your batting order as I have done on the illustrated score-sheet.

Then, at random, you select a passage from a book, a magazine or a newspaper. To give you the idea, I have picked the first two printed lines of a very interesting book entitled 'They Made Cricket' by G. D. Martineau. These are the lines:

'The game of cricket began in a trivial, haphazard

fashion, as a children's pastime. At that stage it must have . . .'

And that is sufficient to commence play – with Adams facing the bowling of Watt. The first letter in the selected passage is 't' which has a value of 4 runs – four to Adams and –remember this – 4 runs conceded by Watt the bowler. Adams scores two runs off the next letter 'h' and one off the third letter 'e'. And that one run means, of course, that his batting partner, Baker, now faces Watt's fourth ball. The letter is 'g' – two runs to Baker. He fails to score off the next ball – the letter 'a' – but strokes a nice boundary for four off Watt's last ball of the over (the letter 'm' in the word 'game').

End of the over and it is Adams facing the first ball from Young – and the letter 'e'. That scores one run for Adams and brings Baker to the batting end. The letters 'o' and then 'f' see Baker scoring two and three runs respectively and brings Adams to face Young's fourth ball of his first over. We have covered the words 'the game of' and the next letter is 'c' – and that means that Adams is 'out' – caught off the bowling of Young. (The 'captain' of the bowling side can nominate anyone he likes as the player who took the catch.)

So the game continues with Cook coming in to face Young. The first letter for him is 'r' – two runs, but there is no scoring stroke to the last ball of the over – the letter 'i', so Baker now faces the first ball of Watt's second over. It is the letter 'c' and Baker is caught out. Davies comes in and gets off the mark immediately with a boundary for four (letter 'k'), followed by a single (letter 'e') that brings Cook down to face Watt. He gets four for the letter 't' but is out next ball – clean bowled by Watt (the letter 'b').

Three wickets have fallen for 30 runs and Edwards the incoming batsman has one more ball to face of Watt's second over. It is the letter 'e' – a single to get Edwards off the mark and ready to face Young . . .

I expect by now you have got the idea. I have completed the innings in my example.

BATSMAN	RUNS	HOW OUT	
1 Adams	4·2·1·1 /	c.Smith b YOUNG	8
2 Baker	2·4·2·3 /	c.Rose b WATT	11
3 Cook	2·4 /	bowled WATT	6
4 Davies	4·1·1·4·2·6·2·2·2·1·2 /	bowled YOUNG	27
5 Edwards	1·2·1 /	l.b.w. bowled YOUNG	4
6 Fox	2·3·6·2·2·3·2·2·2·1·2 /	c.Rose b.THOMAS	27
7 Green		bowled THOMAS	0
8 Hardy	/	l.b.w bowled THOMAS	0
9 Iremy	1 /	st.Rose b THOMAS	1
10 Jones		NOT OUT	0
11 King	4·1·4·4 /	bowled YOUNG	13
Extras			0
			97

(Adams) (Baker) (Cook) (Edwards)
Fall of wickets: 1 for 19; 2 for 21; 3 for 30; 4 for 47
5 for 76; 6 for 76; 7 for 76; 8 for 84; 9 for 84
(Fox) (Green) (Hardy) (Davies) (Iremy)

Bowling Analysis

							O	M	R	W
WATT	4 2 1 2 ·4	W4 1 4 W1	4 2 ·6 ··	6· 2 2 3·			4	0	48	2
YOUNG	1 2 5W 2·	2· 1· 1·	W2 ·3 2·	2 2 ·2 1·	2 2 1 1 2W	4 4 W	5.3	0	42	4
THOMAS	2· WW ·W	·W ·4 1·					2	0	7	4

30. A TEST PAPER

1. What was the name of the bowler who, playing for Australia against England, took the first hat-trick in Test cricket?

2. Who, four years later, was the first English bowler to achieve a hat-trick in Test cricket?

3. Who, also playing for Australia, scored the very first century in Test cricket?

4. Who was the first Englishman to score a century in a Test match?

5. Time passes – and who, many years later, was the West Indian batsman who scored a century in each of five consecutive Test innings?

6. Another West Indian batsman of the same period scored five centuries – not consecutively but in the same Test series. Who was he?

7. What is the lowest total recorded by England in a completed Test innings?

8. What is the lowest total recorded by Australia in a complete Test innings?

9. Only one wicket-keeper in Test cricket to date has made more than 300 dismissals. Can you name him?

10. Only one bowler to date has taken more than 300 Test wickets. Can you name him?

31. ALL IN THE FAMILY

1. What was the surname of the brothers, Dennis and Leslie, who played cricket for Middlesex and football for the Arsenal?

2. Not to be outdone by those Middlesex brothers, the Surrey side of the time was proud of their 'twins' – one of whom is still very active in the cricket world. Can you name the twins?

3. The Steele brothers: one plays for Leicestershire and one for Northamptonshire. What are their first names and who plays for which county?

4. Two brothers are regular members of the current Australian Test side. Can you name them and say which of them is the Australian captain?

5. Sussex is a county club with frequent family connecnections. What was the surname of the brothers John and James who contributed so much to cricket from the 1920s to the 1950s? John, later to become a first-class umpire, scored 34,380 runs in his career. James scored about 2,500 less runs but he also took 1,530 wickets.

6. In recent seasons, brothers Tony and Mike have rendered good service to Sussex. What is their surname?

7. Wallace Hadlee was a famous post-war New Zealand Test player. Now two of his sons play for New Zealand in Test cricket. Can you name them?

8. D. J. S. and M. N. S. Taylor are brothers currently playing in County cricket. (a) For what counties respectively? (b) The initial 'S' stands for the same name for each brother. What name?

9. The two Tolchard brothers play for (a) what county? (b) What are their first names? and (c) which of them is the wicket-keeper?

32. THE FIGHT FOR THE ASHES

1. The first-ever Test match was played between Australia and England in Melbourne. In what year?

2. What are 'The Ashes' and who were the first holders of 'The Ashes'?

3. In a Test series of *five* matches between England and Australia has one country ever won all five matches? If so, which country and when?

4. When did Australia gain the Ashes for the first time?

5. In England in 1934, the touring Australians regained the Ashes they had lost 18 months earlier when D. R. Jardine's team won four of five matches played in Australia. Who was captain of the 1934 Australian tourists?

6. England did not regain the Ashes until 1953 when, in England, they won once and four matches were drawn. Who captained England then and on the 1954-55 tour of Australia when the Ashes were retained?

7. Australia regained the Ashes during England's 1958-59 tour, with one match drawn and four Australian victories. (a) Who captained Australia and (b) headed their batting averages for the series?

8. Australia then retained the Ashes touring England in (a) 1961 (b) 1964 and (c) 1968, and playing at home in (d) 1962-63 and (e) 1956-66. Can you name the five captains of the *tourists*?

9. England regained the Ashes in Australia in 1970-71. Who was the England captain?

33. COUNTY BADGES – 4

For each badge can you fill in (a) the name of the county, (b) the county colours and (c) a description of the badge?

34. AN AUSTRALIAN TEAM

The Australian equivalent to our County Championship is the annual round of matches between State XIs for the Sheffield Shield. Five States compete – Queensland, Western Australia, New South Wales, Victoria and South Australia and the Australian selectors look to the Sheffield Shield matches when choosing players for the national team. Below is a possible Australian national team. Can you (a) complete the names of the eleven players and the 12th man and (b) add the name of the State for which each player plays?

State

1. Ian R – – – – – – ....

2. 'The General' McC – – – – – ....

3. Ian C – – – – – – – ....

4. Ross E – – – – – – ....

5. G – – – Chappell ....

6. Rodney M – – – – ....

7. A. A. M – – – – – – ....

8. K. J. O'K – – – – ....

9. G – – – – Dymock ....

10. Max W– – – – – ....

11. Jeff T – – – – – – ....

12. Wally E – – – – – – ....

To give you a clue – Queensland and Western Australia each supplied three players, and the remaining States two players each.

35. FIND THE COUNTY

All the players listed below have played for England in Test cricket. Each set of them played for the same county. Can you name the county and also say what the players had in common in Test cricket. Were they, for instance, all captains, or wicket-keepers, opening bats, quick bowlers, etc.?

1. W. Rhodes, H. Sutcliffe, L. Hutton, G. Boycott

2. M. C. Cowdrey, A. P. F. Chapman, Hon. Ivo Bligh, Lord Harris

3. L. E. G. Ames, T. G. Evans, W. H. V. Levett, A. P. E. Knott

4. R. Abel, J. B. Hobbs, T. Hayward, A. Sandham

5. D. C. S. Compton, W. J. Edrich, E. Hendren, J. W. Hearne

6. H. Wood, R. Swetman, H. Strudwick

7. A. V. Bedser, P. Loader, G. G. Arnold

8. A. Shrewsbury, A. O. Jones, A. Shaw

9. A. C. MacLaren, H. Makepeace, J. T. Tyldesley, C. Washbrook

10. J. Lillywhite, A. E. R. Gilligan, E. R. Dexter, C. A. Smith

36. WE ARE THE CHAMPIONS

1. The most successful three counties have won the County Championship outright on (a) 31 (b) 18 and (c) 12 occasions. Can you name the three counties?

2. Two counties have won the Championship outright twice – and only twice. Which two?

3. One county can lay claim to one Championship victory – it was gained in 1936. Which county?

4. Five of the 17 first-class counties contesting the Championship have yet to win the title. How many of them can you name?

5. The championship title has been shared in seven seasons – once (in 1889) by three counties. Which county has been most often concerned in shared titles?

6. The title was last shared in 1950. Which county since then has won the most championships?

7. The championship was won by the same county in seven consecutive seasons. Which county? And over what seasons?

8. In 1914 the leading three batsmen in the averages were (a) J. W. Hearne (b) J. B. Hobbs and (c) C. P. Mead. For which counties were they playing?

9. In 1954 the leading three batsmen in the averages were (a) D. C. S. Compton (b) T. W. Graveney and (c) T. L. Livingstone. For which counties were they playing?

37. WINNING COUNTIES

If you can solve this coded diagram you will find the names of two counties (omitting the 'shire' at the end of each name). Both won cricket competitions in 1974. Which counties? Which competitions?

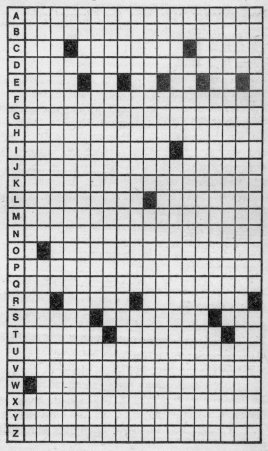

38. GREAT NAMES IN CRICKET – 4

The first of our 'Great Names in Cricket' made his first-class debut with the beginning of the County Championship in 1864 and continued his career in first-class cricket until 1908. Three years before, our third 'Great Name' had made his first appearances for Surrey. He continued to play for Surrey until 1934, and it was in that season that our great cricketer No. 4 started his first-class career with his native county, Yorkshire.

His first innings in first-class cricket was not exactly a success – he was dismissed without scoring! Overall, however, when he retired in 1957, he had scored a total of 40,051 runs in first-class matches – with an average of 55.54 and a proud tally of 129 centuries.

No. 4 was born in Pudsey, Yorkshire in 1916. His son, Richard, was also born there in 1942 and, like his father, played for Yorkshire – and for England. Our player made his Test debut against New Zealand at Lords in 1937 – three days after his 21st birthday. That ought to have been something to celebrate but, sadly, he was clean-bowled for a duck in the first innings – on a good wicket on which England scored 424 runs.

His whole career was to be characterised by the dedicated determination shown by many other Yorkshire players before and after him. A month later, in the Second Test at Manchester, he revealed what was to be his true merit as an England opener by scoring the first of his 19 Test match centuries.

It was a year later, when the Australians were the touring team in England, that he first made his mark in Test match records. The first two Test matches in the 1938 series had been drawn and the third abandoned at Manchester before the Australians, with Bill O'Reilly taking 5 for 66 and 5 for 56 in England's two innings and Don Bradman contributing his usual century, won the Fourth Test at Headingley, Leeds.

England had to win the Fifth Test at the Oval to tie the series. They batted first and amassed the formidable total of 903 for 7 wickets declared. Our mystery player's individual score was 364 runs – beating the then record for an individual record in a Test match innings (set by Wally Hammond when he scored 336 not out for England in Auckland against New Zealand in April 1933).

Not only had our player set the record for the most runs scored by a single batsman in a Test match innings – he had been at the wicket for 800 minutes, a longer time than any previous Test batsman.

Both records were to last for nearly twenty years and then both were beaten in the same Test series but by two different batsmen. The series was between the Pakistani tourists and the West Indies. In the First Test in Barbados, Hanif Mohammad scored 337 runs but the record he established was being at the wicket for 16 hours and ten minutes – nearly 1,000 minutes!

That match was drawn. The West Indians won the Second Test in Trinidad. A promising batsman named Gary Sobers, then 21 years of age, had made his first Test appearance four years before but had still to score his first Test century. He came to the wicket when the West Indies' first wicket fell at 87. He was still there when the innings was declared closed at 790 runs for 3 wickets. The declaration had been held back until his own score had reached 365 not out – the new record. He had made the runs in 608 minutes.

Our player did not score his runs at that rate but, despite any injury to his left arm during war service, from 1937 until 1954 he was a reliable opener for England. More, he was honoured in 1952 by becoming the first professional in modern cricket to captain England. He never let England down and his final test record was a total of 6,971 runs scored in 138 innings in 79 Test matches. Later he was knighted for his services to cricket. Who was he?

39. SIX OF A KIND

The words below are the jumbled up names of six cricketers. To help you discover which player in each case I have added the name of the county for which he played in the 1974 season.

When you have solved these anagrams, can you say what it is that these six players have in common?

1. BLIND STORE CHASER . . . .
                    (Leicestershire)

2. SCAN IRE LOB   . . . .
                              (Somerset)

3. DRY OAR BOW   . . . .
                              (Lancashire)

4. JEWISH BAR KNACK   . . . .
                              (Leicestershire)

5. STAY BARRED   . . . .
                              (Nottinghamshire)

6. SEEMED MILKY   . . . .
                              (Nottinghamshire)

40. NAMESAKES

Some cricketers have had the same surname as famous men of the past. Here are some of them – with *their* initials not those of their notable namesakes. Can you say for which county – in the case of those marked (a), or which country – marked (b), they played cricket?

Men of History

1. (a) Julius Caesar

2. (b) H. Moses

3. (a) R. Abel

4. (a) T. L. Livingstone

5. (b) J. S. Solomon

Men of Letters

6. (a) L. H. Tennyson

7. (b) P. S. Heine

8. (a) G. G. Arnold

9. (a) G. G. Macaulay

10. (b) A. Melville

41. FIELDING – 3

A third typical field placing is illustrated below (as in
Puzzles 14 and 24). Again we have a fast or medium
paced right-hand bowler, but the important difference is
that this is not the field for a County Championship match
but for one of limited overs as the 40-overs matches in
the John Player League or, to a slightly lesser extent, the
60-overs matches in the Gillette and Benson & Hedges
Cup competitions. Can you mark in the names of the fielding positions and say why this field setting is so different
from that shown in either Puzzle 14 or Puzzle 24?

42. THEN AND NOW

Then

1. What cricketer, born in May 1874, scored 157 runs in an hour against the West Indies in 1900; 101 out of 118 in 40 minutes' playing for Gloucestershire against Yorkshire in 1897; and – finest of all – 104 out of 139 in 75 minutes for England against Australia in 1902?
2. Who was the Surrey amateur who, playing against Northampton in 1920, scored 113 not out (of 171 runs scored whilst he was at the wicket) in 42 minutes? He reached his century in 35 minutes.
3. The most runs (345) in one day by a batsman was scored at Nottingham in 1921 by an Australian batting for the tourists against the county. Who was he?
4. An Australian also holds the record for the fastest Test century. He made it in 70 minutes on Australia's 1921-22 tour of South Africa. Can you name him?

Now – the 1974 season in England

5. With their first innings limited to 100 overs and their first wicket falling before a run had been scored, Warwickshire playing against Gloucestershire, had scored 465 for one when their overs ran out. Both scoring batsmen scored double centuries. Who were they?
6. Lancashire batting second and with 118 overs at their disposal recorded the highest championship innings of the season. They totalled 480 for six and two batsmen scored centuries – one of them a career-best. Who were they?
7. Between the first two Tests, Pakistan played at Eastbourne against a D. H. Robins XI. In that match a Hampshire batsman scored 273 not out against the tourists in 252 minutes with 13 sixes and 31 fours. Can you name him?
8. Who scored a century in 83 minutes for Nottinghamshire against Derbyshire in August 1974?

Illustrated below are another three badges. Can you fill in (a) the name of the county, (b) the county colours and (c) a description of the badge?

44. SOME SLIPS

Soon after each English cricket season ends those daily newspapers, whose coverage of sport extends beyond the news, preferably sensationally presented, of the day, begin printing the County cricket averages. Cricket lovers glance at them and remember pleasant afternoons in the sun; but how closely do they look at the averages? Close enough to notice mistakes, usually printing ones, that creep in? It was only because I needed to check and re-check a few times to prepare the statistics at the end of this book that I noticed some of these mistakes.

Here is how two papers printed some batting averages. Can you see, almost at a glance, which paper was correct in each case?

1. R. D. V. Knight, Gloucestershire.

	Matches	Innings	Times not out	Runs	Ave.
Paper A:	19	33	5	1,196	42.71
Paper B:	19	33	5	950	42.71

2. J. N. Shepherd, Kent

	Matches	Innings	Times not out	Runs	Ave.
Paper A:	18	25	5	513	25.65
Paper B:	18	25	5	513	26.65

3. M. J. Harris, Notts.

	Matches	Innings	Times not out	Runs	Ave.
Paper A:	19	35	3	1,431	31.30
Paper B:	19	35	3	1,431	44.71

4. D. W. Randall, Notts.

	Matches	Innings	Times not out	Runs	Ave.
Paper A:	18	34	4	639	31.30
Paper B:	18	34	4	639	21.30

And here are two averages printed in the papers that obviously are incorrect. Can you spot what is wrong?

5. M. J. Smedley, Notts. – *batting*

20 matches, 36 innings, 6 times not out, 1,059 runs, 18 not out highest score. Average 35.30

6. N. Gifford, Worcs. – *bowling*

57.3 overs, 185 maidens, 1,215 runs, 66 wickets. Ave. 18.40

45. AN A–Z OF PLAYERS OF TODAY

A is for .... Warwickshire batsman whose great innings of 262 not out in Kingston kept alive England's chances against the West Indies, 1973–74

B is for .... Skippered Lancashire to three successive Gillette Cup Final wins

C is for .... The Lancashire, Surrey, Lancashire again, and now Worcestershire cricketer who has played professional football as goalkeeper for Tranmere Rovers, West Bromwich Albion and Aston Villa

D is for .... The Scots-born captain of England against the West Indies, India, Pakistan and Australia in 1973–74–75

E is for .... Promising Middlesex slow left arm bowler and former captain of Cambridge University. Born in Lusaka, the capital of Zambia

F is for .... 1972 Oxford Blue and made his debut for the county of his birth, Sussex, in 1973. Maiden century in 1974. Grandson of former Prime Minister, Harold Macmillan

G is for .... Either Gordon or Geoffrey will do. Both were born in Barbados and now play in England for southern counties

H is for .... The Yorkshire and England cricketer with a 'county' name

I is for .... Former England captain who was awarded the CBE in the 1973 New Year Honours List

J is for .... India-born Surrey bowler – and no mean batsman. Capped for his county in 1970

K is for .... Cambridge Blue like his father before him but he plays Test cricket for Pakistan. Father played for India. Plays county cricket for Glamorgan

L is for .... Lancashire and England fast bowler – born in Yorkshire in the 'border town' of Todmorden

M is for .... Middlesex and England wicket-keeper who, in 1957, completed the 'wicket-keeper's double' of 1,000 runs and 100 dismissals

N is for .... Popular Yorkshire fast-medium bowler who made his debut in 1962, was capped a year later and had his benefit year in 1973

O is for .... Yorkshire and England fast bowler and brother of England rugger international

P is for .... Somerset player who played for Sussex, as his father had done, from 1949 to 1972. Made 46 Test match appearances for England

Q is for   A Warwick and Worcester player of long ago and the only player with a surname beginning with the letter 'Q' to play in a Test

R is for .... Hampshire's express bowler from Antigua who headed the first-class bowling averages in 1974 – and his first full season in English cricket

S is for .... Glamorgan's all-rounder who was born in Dar-es-Salaam

T is for .... Worcestershire's attractive New Zealand opening bat who scored over 1,000 runs by the end of May in 1973

U is for .... Kent and England bowler who took 100 wickets in his debut season (1936) and has been taking wickets galore ever since

V is for .... Taunton-born and Somerset player from 1957 to 1972. Now with Northamptonshire and the batsman who scored the most runs in first-class cricket in England in 1974

W is for .... Warwickshire, formerly Surrey, fast bowler who was born in Sunderland. Made his Test debut in England's 1970–71 tour of Australia

X is for Mr Extras

Y is for .... Popular Pakistani batsman who has played for Surrey since 1965 – capped in 1969

Z is for .... Gloucestershire player since 1972 and much missed in that county's 1974 matches when he was on duty for Pakistan – amongst other fine innings scoring 240 runs in an innings against England

46. BEST WITH BAT AND BALL – 3

In the 1974 County Championship matches who →

1. Headed Nottinghamshire's batting averages list? His average was 48.6, with a total of 1,110 runs scored.

2. Scored the most runs for Glamorgan – 1,104 of them?

3. Took the most wickets as a bowler for Surrey? 79 of them

4. Headed the batting averages for Leicestershire? He had 30 completed innings and a total of 1,392 runs.

5. Took 54 wickets for Kent – the most of any Kent player?

6. Had the best bowling analysis (17.18 average for 39 wickets) for Gloucestershire?

7. With an average of 39.48 and 1,224 runs, headed Sussex's batting averages?

8. Headed Somerset's bowling averages list with 65 wickets taken and an average of 19.01?

9. Took the most wickets (82 of them) for Warwickshire?

10. With an average of 18.12 and 55 wickets taken, headed Northamptonshire's bowling averages list?

47. SOME FAMOUS BOWLERS

In the following list of 15 Test cricketers, all selected as bowlers, four played for Australia, four for England, two Pakistan, two for the West Indies; and one for each of India, New Zealand and South Africa. Can you complete the table by entering the name of the country for which each played, and ticking under the period (or periods) in which the player appeared in *Test matches*?

	Country	A Up to 1914	B 1919- 39	C 1946- 66	D 1967- 1974
1. Bishen Bedi	....	...	...	...	...
2. Richie Benaud	....	...	...	...	...
3. Lance Gibbs	....	...	...	...	...
4. Clarrie Grimmett	....	...	...	...	...
5. Jack Gregory	....	...	...	...	...
6 Fazal Mahmood	....	...	...	...	...
7. Tony MacGibbon	....	...	...	...	...
8. Bill O'Reilly	....	...	...	...	...
9. Sonny Ramadhin	....	...	...	...	...
10. Wilfred Rhodes	....	...	...	...	...
11. Safraz Narwaz	....	...	...	...	...
12. John Snow	....	...	...	...	...
13. Hugh Tayfield	....	...	...	...	...
14. Freddie Trueman	....	...	...	...	...
15. Hedley Verity	....	...	...	...	...

48. GREAT NAMES IN CRICKET – 5

I don't suppose there were many schoolboys in the 1930's who did not see themselves as 'the Don' when they set up their pile of coats as wickets on the waste ground. Yet sometimes sheer loyalty persuaded us to spurn the Australian Bradman and to 'be' instead the Dover-born (in 1903) cricketer who played in 85 Test matches for England from 1927 (51 runs against South Africa at Johannesburg on his debut) to 1947 (79 runs against New Zealand at Christchurch in his final Test innings).

His Test career batting average falls well below that of Bradman's 99.94 but that is true of all players, and our player can lay claim to a very useful tally of 83 wickets as a Test match bowler for an average of 37.83. And he was also one of the greatest slip fielders of all time.

His county was Gloucestershire and he made his first appearance for it in 1920. In 1927 he became only the second batsman to score 1,000 runs in first-class matches played before the end of May. It was in the 1930s that he so often dominated the batting averages – 1st in 1933 (when he scored 3,323 runs in 54 innings), 3rd in 1934, 1st in the three seasons 1935, 1936 and 1937, 2nd to Bradman in 1938 and to George Headley in 1939.

He had turned amateur in 1937 and was appointed captain of Gloucestershire (he also captained England) in 1939. He remained captain when first-class cricket was resumed after the Second World War in 1946 – and finished that season top of the batting averages. He then led England on the 1946–47 tour of Australia and New Zealand. His Test match runs totalled 7,249 – only Gary Sobers and Colin Cowdrey have scored more runs in Test cricket.

In all first class matches he scored over 50,000 runs with an average of 56.10, and including 167 centuries.

Can you identify him?

49. TRUE OR FALSE?

1. The Nawab of Pataudi, father of the present Indian captain (against the West Indies in 1974/75), played Test cricket for both England and India.

2. The famous Australian bowler, Clarrie Grimmett, was born in New Zealand.

3. Apart from the present 17 counties, no other county has ever taken part in the County Cricket Championship.

4. Wally Hammond played for England in Test cricket both before and after the Second World War.

5. Jack Hobbs scored more centuries in County Championship matches than any other player.

6. On each of the four occasions when he toured England, Don Bradman headed the all-comers list of batting averages for the season.

7. George Headley, father of the present Worcestershire batsman, made his Test debut for the West Indies against England and in the course of the series scored four centuries.

8. Of the England party who set off in October 1974 to tour Australia and New Zealand, the most capped player was Alan Knott.

9. Hampshire's fast bowler, Andy Roberts, had not appeared for his country, the West Indies, in a Test match when he made his County Championship debut in 1974.

10. Worcestershire were the first winners of the Gillette Cup.

50: THE LIMITED OVERS GAME

1. First of the sponsored limited-over competitions was the Gillette Cup. In which of these years was it first competed for? (a) 1960 (b) 1963 (c) 1964 (d) 1966.

2. Which is the only county to have won the Gillette Cup in three successive seasons?

3. Second in seniority of the sponsored competitions is the John Player League – so popular with spectators and tele-viewers on summer Sundays. In what season was the League first competed for?

4. Two counties have won the John Player League Championship on two occasions. Can you name them?

5. In what season was the Benson and Hedges Cup competition started?

6. Who were the first winners of the Benson and Hedges Cup?

Remember the 1974 season . . .

7. The quarter-finals of the 1974 Gillette Cup were played between (a) Somerset and Surrey (b) Kent and Leicestershire (c) Lancashire and Yorkshire and (d) Nottinghamshire and Worcestershire. Which four qualified for the semi-finals?

8. Who were the two players who scored centuries in the 1974 Gillette Cup quarter-final matches?

9. The quarter-finals of the 1974 Benson & Hedges Cup were played between (a) Kent and Leicestershire (b) Hampshire and Somerset (c) Lancashire and Worcestershire and (d) Surrey and Yorkshire. Which four won?

10. The eight innings of the 1974 Benson and Hedges quarter-finals included only one century-maker. Who was he?

51. FIELDING – 4

In the field setting illustrated below, the match is one of limited-overs similar to the match illustrated in Puzzle 41, but in this case the bowler is a slow bowler. As with the other field-setting puzzles, can you mark in the names of the fielding positions? What changes have been made compared with the fast bowler's field setting illustrated in Puzzle 41?

52. A FEW BUMPERS

1. Who is accepted as being the inventor of 'The Googly'?

2. Who was the 'head and the right arm' of the Hambledon Cricket Club?

3. In which Test match were brothers on opposing sides? Two of them were in the same side and a third in the opposition side.

4. In the same match, two members of England's team, W. L. Murdoch and J. J. Ferris, had previously played for another country. Which one and against whom?

5. The longest-ever Test match was played between South Africa and England at Durban in March 1939. How many days did it last and what was the result?

6. What have these six bowlers in common. A. Coningham (Australia 1894–5), G. G. Macaulay (England 1922–23), M. W. Tate (England 1924), T. Johnson (West Indies 1939), R. Howorth (England 1947) and Intikhab Alam (Pakistan 1959–60).

7. Only one player has appeared for both England and Australia in Test matches between those two countries. Can you name him?

8. Who was out 'obstructing the field' in the Test match between England and South Africa at the Oval in 1951?

9. Who was the youngest player to play for England in a Test match?

10. Who was out 'handled ball' playing for South Africa against England at Cape Town during the 1956–57 series of Test matches?

53. STALEMATE AGAINST PAKISTAN

The 1974 series of Test matches against Pakistan had promised to be one of the most exciting series of recent years. In the event that old bugbear of cricket – RAIN – so interfered with play that all three matches were drawn. But there were many bits of good cricket, and many interesting features. How much can you remember of the series?

1. On what ground was the first Test match of the series played? In what town?
2. Who made his first Test match appearance for Pakistan in the match?
3. Thanks largely to a fine tail-ender's innings of 53 by Sarfraz, Pakistan's first innings totalled 285 runs. Who was their top scorer?
4. In the Second Test, Pakistan had barely settled in to build their first innings when a sudden thunderstorm burst over the ground and soaked the wicket. When play was resumed one of the English bowlers was almost unplayable. Pakistan declare at 130 for nine. Who was the England bowler who had taken 5 for 20?
5. England also struggled to begin with and had one of their lower batsmen to thank for their total of 270. He scored 83 of the runs. Who was he?
6. On what grounds were (a) the Second and (b) the Third Tests played?
7. Pakistan again batted first in the Third Test and scored a massive 600 for 7 declared. One of their batsmen scored 240 – it was only the second time he had scored a Test century. He was . . . ?
8. England's reply, which lasted until the fifth day, finally reached 545 runs. Keith Fletcher contributed 122. Who was the bowler who scored 65?

54. COUNTY BADGES – 6

Here are the remaining three badges for you to identify. Can you fill in (a) the name of the county, (b) the county colours and (c) a description of the badge?

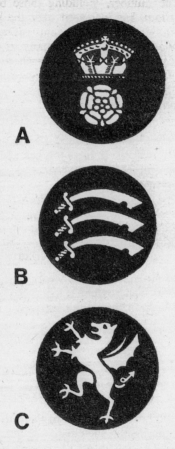

A

B

C

55. IMPORTS AND EXPORTS

Yorkshire have always sought to maintain their tradition of fielding sides composed wholly of Yorkshire-born players but 'strangers' have always appeared in most other county sides. The number, including those born outside the United Kingdom, has increased over the years. Here, picked at random, are two 1974 county sides, fielded by Somerset and Worcestershire. How many of the players were (a) born in the county (b) born elsewhere in the U.K. (c) born outside the U.K.? (It is an interesting exercise that you can try with other counties too.)

SOMERSET		WORCESTERSHIRE	
Player	*Where Born*	*Player*	*Where Born*
M. J. Kitchen	....	R. G. A. Headley	....
D. J. S. Taylor	....	G. M. Turner	....
G. Burgess	....	J. A. Ormrod	....
V. Richards	....	J. M. Parker	....
D. B. Close	....	B. L. D'Oliveira	....
J. M. Parks	....	T. J. Yardley	....
I. T. Botham	....	H. G. Wilcock	....
D. Breakwell	....	N. Gifford	....
B. A. Langford	....	V. A. Holder	....
H. Moseley	....	J. D. Inchmore	....
A. A. Jones	....	B. M. Brain	....

56. CARELESS STROKES

What one deliberate mistake has the writer made in each of the following incidents?

A. It was in the second innings of that famous cricket match, played in 1775 on the Artillery Ground between Five of Kent and Five of Hambledon, that 'Lumpy' Stevens had his revenge when he bowled John Small by knocking out his middle stump.

B. In those 22 days from 9th–30th May, 1895, W. G. Grace had amassed 1,016 runs. He was then in his 47th year. Small wonder that when, later in the season, he appeared at Lord's, the crowd in the Mound Stand rose, like one man, to applaud him as he walked to the wicket.

C. No one who witnessed it will ever forget Jessop's memorable innings at the Oval in August 1902. England were in trouble, but from the moment that broad, sturdy frame descended the steps and advanced to the wicket, an air of expectancy swept around the ground. The opposing captain waved his fielders back towards the boundary. Then silence as The Croucher bent low over his bat. Soon the score was mounting. He had made 44 when, effortlessly it seemed, he swung his bat at the next ball. It cleared the boundary – and was 'caught' by a happy spectator! Another six to add to the three he had already scored with similar strokes.

57. PLAYING AT HOME

Which counties would you expect to find playing at home on the following grounds?

1. Headingley

2. Trent Bridge

3. Nevill Cricket Ground

4. The Oval

5. Saffrons Cricket Ground

6. Grace Road Cricket Ground

7. Old Trafford

8. Sophia Gardens

9. Lords

10. Edgbaston

And who would be entertaining a county XI –

11. at Fenners?

12. in the Parks?

He was born in 1904, played all his County cricket for
Nottinghamshire, headed the national bowling averages on
five occasions between 1927 and 1936, and once, in that
period, finished third in the averages. He played in only
21 Test matches – eleven at home, and his overseas tours
were limited to two. Both tours were to Australia – in
1928–29 and, most remembered, in 1932–33.

He was a fast bowler but, unlike the majority of fast
bowlers, he was a comparatively small man with a beauti-
fully balanced run-up and delivery, and with deadly
accuracy. However, his first Test match appearances –
twice against the visiting Australians in 1926 – gave no hint
of the storm that was to come. His next appearances –
again in only two of the three Tests played – were against
the West Indies in 1928. His best performance was in the
second West Indian innings in Third Test when he took
three wickets for 41 runs.

Then, in 1928–29, he toured Australia and played two
important roles in England's win by 675 runs in the First
Test. As a batsman – showing skill in Test matches that
he had less opportunity to show in county matches – he
shared with Patsy Hendren in what remains as England's
record 8th wicket partnership against the Australians – 124
runs. As a bowler he captured six Aussie wickets in their
first innings for 32 runs. It was a great series for England
with four wins to Australia's one.

The Australians, with the young Bradman amongst them
for the first time on tour in England, came to England in
1930 – and recaptured the Ashes by winning two matches
to England's one (two matches were drawn). The scene was
set for England's revenge when they returned to Australia
for the 1932–33 series. The captain was D. R. Jardine and
the tactic was to attack the Australian batsmen with fast
bowlers, spearheaded by our player, directing their fire

at the leg stump. England won the First Test at Sydney by ten wickets with our player taking 5 for 96 in the first innings and 5 for 28 in the second.

Australia won the Second Test but England won the final three Tests in a row. A great victory, but one which was accompanied on the cricket grounds by roars of abuse from the spectators and off the pitches by all manner of diplomatic wrangling. The English fast bowlers, and our player in particular, were accused of 'bodyline' bowling. It had been an amazingly successful series for him. In his entire Test career of 21 matches he took 78 wickets (for the good Test match average of 28.41) but in the 1932–33 series of five Test matches he captured 33 of them. And, as if to doubly antagonise the spectators, he also shone in the final Test as a batsman, scoring 98 runs in England's first innings of 454. A pity those final two runs eluded him.

All the more a pity because, partly in consequence of a foot injury but also because of the intense hostility aroused by England's alleged 'bodyline' tactics, he did not play in another Test match.

However, there remained a happy and surprising ending to his Australian connections. No-one, except perhaps the England captain D. R. Jardine, could have been more reviled by cricket-mad Australians than he was in 1933. Yet, after the Second World War, it was to Australia that he emigrated. It was in Australia that his family grew up and where he celebrated his seventieth birthday around the time that the 1974–75 touring English party prepared to play Australia in the First Test.

Maybe those who saw him play retain different recollections – Australians who were boys in 1932, recall their batting heroes drawing away from that red ball he had hurtled towards them; Englishmen who were boys then, recall his rhythmic delivery and the sustained accuracy – but no-one would deny him his place amongst the Great Names in Cricket.

Who was he?

59. COMPLETE THE NAMES

More cricketers with three given names in addition to their surnames. These are all post-war players – many of them are still playing in first-class cricket. Can you identify them and complete their surnames?

1. K. W. R. F – – – – – – – Essex captain and an England player since 1968

2. D. C. S. C – – – – – – Prolific Middlesex and England run-getter – and an Arsenal footballer

3. E. J. O. H – – – – – – Another footballer/cricketer – still playing today for Sheffield United and Worcestershire

4. P. B. H. M – – Surrey and England captain and elegant batsman

5. A. C. D. I-M – – – – – – – – Hampshire captain when that county first won the Championship

6. R. M. C. G – – – – – – Hampshire captain when that county won the Championship for the second time

7. G. R. J. R – – – – Surrey all-rounder of today

8. M. J. K. S – – – – Former England captain. First played for Leicestershire before settling with Warwickshire. Played rugger for England.

72

60. READING THE SCORE CARD

Unfortunately the number of runs scored by three of the batsmen have been left out by the printer. In this case, however that does not matter because there is enough information printed for their scores to be inserted. Can you work out the missing scores?

1.	Hamilton	lbw b Jones	
2.	Garwood	c Smith b Jackson ...	10
3.	Hopkins	st Green b Brown ...	
4.	Talbot	c and b Brown	24
5.	Pelham	c Gray b Jackson ...	46
6.	Penn	b Jones	
7.	Swift	c Davies b Brown ...	3
8.	Snook	b Brown	0
9.	Carter	st Green b Brown ...	6
10.	Rogers	lbw b Jones	13
11.	Hooper	not out	4
		Extras	0
			184

Fall of wickets: 1 for 0; 2 for 22; 3 for 22; 4 for 62; 5 for 112; 6 for 125; 7 for 130; 8 for 144; 9 for 174.

61. A BIT OF A TEST

1. What is the highest aggregate of runs recorded in one Test match?

2. What is the highest score recorded in one Test match innings?

3. What is the lowest aggregate of runs recorded in a completed Test match?

4. What is the record victory in Test cricket by an innings margin?

5. What is the largest number of centuries scored in a single Test match innings?

6. What is the highest score recorded by Australia in one Test match innings?

7. What is the highest score recorded by the West Indies in one Test match innings?

8. Who was the batsman who, in the course of that record score by the West Indies, scored the highest individual innings in Test cricket?

9. Whose record did he break? It had been made at Kennington Oval in 1938.

10. In the same Test series that saw the records set mentioned in questions 7 and 8, another record was established – that of the longest innings by a batsman in first-class cricket. Who was the batsman, and for how long was he at the wicket?

62. BOWLER TO WICKET

By changing one letter at a time – always to make a recognised word – can you, as the bowler, hit the wicket in two overs (12 balls) or less?

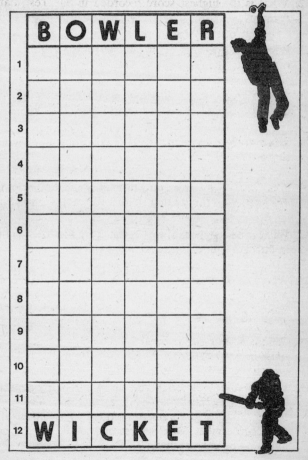

	B	O	W	L	E	R
1						
2						
3						
4						
5						
6						
7						
8						
9						
10						
11						
12	W	I	C	K	E	T

63. DOWN UNDER – ENGLAND IN AUSTRALIA 1974 – 75

1. Rain interfered with the English tourists' early matches in Australia, but, still before the Test series started, their opening batsmen found conditions that suited them at Melbourne when playing against Victoria. They put on 268 runs for the first wicket and each scored a century. Who were the openers?

2. In a minor match against South-East Queensland, also before the Test match series began, one of the English bowlers finished with the remarkable analysis of 3.5 overs 2 maidens 1 run and 5 wickets. Who was he?

3. Injuries to a number of English batsmen, notably John Edrich and David Lloyd, made it necessary for another batsman to be flown out to join the touring party in Melbourne. Who was he? Twenty years before in a Test at Melbourne he had scored 102 out of a total of 191 runs.

4. Who scored the first century in the 1974–75 Test match series between England and Australia?

5. Who was Australia's most successful bowler in England's first innings in the First Test?

6. In England's second innings in the same Test, an Australian bowler took 6 wickets for 46 runs. Can you name him?

7. Who was England's top scorer in their second innings in the First Test?

8. In the Second Test at Perth, an Australian set up a new Test match record, beating one that was previously held by several players – amongst them his grandfather. What was the record? Who set it up? Who was his grandfather?

9. In the Second Test at Perth, England were dismissed for 208 in the first innings and 293 in the second. None of the players in the top half of the batting order reached 50 runs in either innings but in each innings one lower-order batsman did. Can you name the top scorer in (a) the first innings and (b) the second innings?

10. England's captain, Mike Denness, dropped himself for the Fourth Test. Who was the new captain? Had the new captain at any time previously captained England in a Test match?

11. In which of the Test matches played in the 1974–75 series did Australia regain the Ashes?

12. In the Fourth Test, the Australian fast bowler Jeff Thomson brought his tally of wickets in the series to 30. A few days later in India in the Fourth Test match, a West Indian fast bowler, more familiar to English spectators, equalled the West Indian record with 30 wickets in a series against India, and also became the first West Indian to take 12 wickets in any Test match. Who was he?

13. Australia won the Fifth Test in Adelaide by 163 runs. Only one player in the first four innings of the match scored a century. Can you name him?

14. England won the Sixth Test by an innings and four runs. (a) Where was the match played? (b) Who captured six Australian wickets for 38 runs in the first innings? (c) Who was England's top scorer with 188 runs?

64. PLAYING AWAY

Two of the ten players listed below were still playing for the county of their birth in the 1974 season, but the other eight were playing for counties other than the one in which they were born. The counties listed as each player's place of birth and present playing county are all jumbled up. Can you correct them?

Player	County where born	Playing county (1974)
1. Bob Willis	Sussex	Leicestershire
	....	... ...
2. Norman McVicker	Worcestershire	Yorkshire
	....	... ...
3. John Snow	Durham	Lancashire
	....	... ...
4. David Bairstow	Lancashire	Northamptonshire
	....	... ...
5. Stewart Storey	Norfolk	Somerset
	....	... ...
6. John Edrich	Yorkshire	Sussex
	....	... ...
7. David Lloyd	Yorkshire	Surrey
	....	... ...
8. Ray Illingworth	Kent	Surrey
	....	... ...
9. Jim Parks	Lancashire	Warwickshire
	....	... ...
10. John Dye	Sussex	Leicestershire
	....	... ...

65. POINTS AND PERCENTAGES

The County Championship has never been, and perhaps never can be, organized in a way that ensures that each county plays each of the others at home and away in a season. To do this would involve each county in 32 three-day championship matches each season. Over the years, a variety of methods for deciding the relative positions of counties has been used.

In 1897, for example, when 14 counties contested the championship, three of them had a full programme of 26 matches to play, whilst one of them had only 14 matches to play. The method of deciding the Championship was thus to ignore all drawn matches; to subtract the number of matches lost from the number of matches won and, allowing one point for each match won less those lost, to calculate the percentage of points to the number of matches finished. Here, in alphabetical order, is the table showing the number of matches played, finished, won, lost and drawn by each county. Can you complete the number of points and the percentages and, so, if you were a cricket fan in 1897, decide the finishing position of each county?

County	Played	Finished games	Won	Lost	Drawn	Points %age	Finishing Position
Derbyshire	16	9	0	9	7		
Essex	16	9	7	2	7		
Gloucestershire	18	12	7	5	6		
Hampshire	18	11	4	7	7		
Kent	18	12	2	10	6		
Lancashire	26	19	16	3	7		
Leicestershire	14	11	1	10	3		
Middlesex	16	7	3	4	9		
Nottinghamshire	16	7	2	5	9		
Somerset	16	12	3	9	4		
Surrey	26	21	17	4	5		
Sussex	20	11	5	6	9		
Warwickshire	18	7	3	4	11		
Yorkshire	26	18	13	5	8		

1974-75

TEST AND COUNTY RECORDS AND AVERAGES

MCC Test results in Australia and New Zealand
MCC Test results in the West Indies
India's Test results in England
Pakistan's Test results in England
England's overall Test record summarised
County Championship Table
John Player League Table
Gillette Cup Final
Benson and Hedges Cup Final
Top Twenty Batsmen in the Averages
Top Twenty Bowlers in the Averages
Top Six for every County

Note. In the lists of averages –

Batting: M – No. of matches I – No. of innings NO – No. of times not out R – No. of runs HS – Highest score Ave – Average
  (*) An asterisk after the highest score indicates that it was 'not out'.

Bowling: O – No. of overs or part overs bowled M – No. of maiden overs R – No. of runs conceded W – No. of wickets taken Ave – Average.

First Test – Brisbane
AUSTRALIA won by 166 runs
Australia : 1st innings : 309 (I. Chappell 90, G. Chappell
58; Willis 4 – 56)
2nd innings : 288 for 5 dec. (R. Edwards 53,
Walters 62 not out)
England : 1st innings : 265 (Greig 110; Walker 4 – 73)
2nd innings : 166 (Thomson 6 – 46)

Second Test – Perth
AUSTRALIA won by 9 wickets
England : 1st innings : 208 (Knott 51)
2nd innings : 293 (Titmus 61; Thomson 5 – 93)
Australia : 1st innings : 481 (G. Chappell 62, R. Edwards
115, Walters 103)
2nd innings : 23 for one

Third Test – Melbourne
MATCH DRAWN
England : 1st innings : 242 (Knott 52; Thomson 4 – 72)
2nd innings : 244 (Amiss 90, Greig 60; Thomson 4 – 71, Mallett 4– 60)
Australia : 1st innings : 241 (Redpath 55; Willis 5 – 61)
2nd innings : 238 for 8 (G. Chappell 61; Greig
4 – 56)

Fourth Test – Sydney
AUSTRALIA won by 171 runs
Australia : 1st innings : 405 (McCosker 80, I. Chappell
53, G. Chappell 84; Arnold
5 – 86, Greig 4 – 104)
2nd innings : 289 for 4 dec. (Redpath 105,
G. Chappell 144)
England : 1st innings : 295 (Edrich 50, Knott 82; Thomson 4 – 73)
2nd innings : 228 (Greig 54; Mallett 4 – 21)

Fifth Test – Adelaide
AUSTRALIA won by 163 runs
Australia: 1st innings: 304 (Jenner 74, Walters 55; Underwood 7 – 113)
             2nd innings: 272 for 5 dec. (Walters 71, Marsh 55, Redpath 52; Underwood 4 – 102)
England: 1st innings: 172 (Denness 51; Lillee 4 – 49)
             2nd innings: 241 (Knott 106 not out, Fletcher 63; Lillee 4 – 69)

Sixth Test – Melbourne
ENGLAND won by an innings and 4 runs
Australia: 1st innings: 152 (I. Chappell 65; Lever 6 – 38)
             2nd innings: 373 (G. Chappell 102, Redpath 83, McCosker 76, I. Chappell 50; Greig 4 – 88)
England: 1st innings: 529 (Denness 188, Fletcher 146, Greig 89, Edrich 70; Walker 8 – 143)

1975 M.C.C. IN NEW ZEALAND
First Test – Auckland
ENGLAND won by an innings and 83 runs
England: 1st innings: 593 for 6 dec. (Fletcher 216, Denness 181, Edrich 64, Greig 51)
New Zealand: 1st innings: 326 (Parker 121, Morrison 58, Wadsworth 58; Greig 5 – 98)
             2nd innings: 184 (Morrison 58, G. Howarth 51 not out; Greig 5 – 51)

Second Test – Christchurch
MATCH DRAWN
New Zealand: 1st innings: 342 (Turner 98, Wadsworth 58)
England: 1st innings: 272 for 2 (Amiss 164 not out, Denness 59 not out)

ENGLAND (v Australia)

Batting	I	NO	R	HS	Ave
J. H. Edrich	7	1	260	70	43.33
A. W. Greig	11	0	446	110	40.54
A. P. E. Knott	11	1	364	106*	36.40
K. W. R. Fletcher	9	0	324	146	36.00
M. H. Denness	9	0	318	188	35.33
D. Lloyd	8	0	196	49	24.50
D. L. Amiss	9	0	175	90	19.44
M. C. Cowdrey	9	0	165	41	18.33
F. J. Titmus	8	0	138	61	17.25
C. M. Old	3	0	50	43	16.66
R. D. G. Willis	10	5	76	15	15.20
B. W. Luckhurst	4	0	54	27	13.50
D. L. Underwood	9	0	111	30	12.33
P. Lever	3	1	24	14	12.00
M. Hendrick	4	2	12	8*	6.00
G. G. Arnold	7	1	22	14	3.66

Bowling	O	M	R	W	Ave
P. Lever	61	8	214	9	23.77
R. D. G. Willis	140.4	15	522	17	30.70
D. L. Underwood	185	42	595	17	35.00
C. M. Old	51.6	4	210	6	35.00
G. G. Arnold	141.1	22	528	14	37.71
A. W. Greig	167.6	19	681	17	40.05
F. J. Titmus	122.3	30	360	7	51.42
M. Hendrick	34.6	6	119	2	59.50

AUSTRALIA

Batting	I	NO	R	HS	Ave
G. S. Chappell	11	0	608	144	55.27
T. J. Jenner	3	1	100	74	50.00
M. H. N. Walker	8	3	221	41*	44.20
I. R. Redpath	12	1	472	105	42.90
K. D. Walters	11	2	383	103	42.55
R. B. McCosker	5	0	202	80	40.40
I. M. Chappell	12	1	387	90	35.18
R. W. Marsh	11	2	313	55	34.77
R. Edwards	9	1	261	115	32.62
J. R. Thomson	5	2	65	24*	21.66
D. K. Lillee	8	2	88	26	14.66
A. A. Mallett	7	2	61	31	12.20
W. J. Edwards	6	0	68	30	11.33
G. Dymock	2	0	0	0	0.00

Bowling	O	M	R	W	Ave
J. R. Thomson	177.1	34	592	17	17.93
A. A. Mallett	140.6	47	339	17	19.94
D. K. Lillee	182.6	36	596	25	23.84
M. H. N. Walker	218.7	46	684	23	29.73
K. D. Walters	56.3	15	175	5	35.00
T. J. Jenner	42	10	136	3	45.33
G. Dymock	39	6	130	1	130.00
I. Chappell	22	3	83	0	–

1974 M.C.C. IN THE WEST INDIES

First Test– Port of Spain
WEST INDIES won by 7 wickets
England: 1st innings: 131 (Boyce 4 – 42)
                    2nd innings: 393 (Amiss 174, Boycott 93)
West Indies: 1st innings: 392 (Kallicharran 158, Julien
                    86 not out; Pocock 5 – 110)
                    2nd innings: 132 for 3 (Fredericks 65 not
                    out)

Second Test – Kingston
MATCH DRAWN
England: 1st innings: 353 (Boycott 68, Denness 67)
                    2nd innings: 432 for 9 (Amiss 262)
West Indies: 1st innings: 583 (Rowe 120, Fredericks 94,
                    Kallicharran 93, Sobers 57)

Third Test – Bridgetown
MATCH DRAWN
England: 1st innings: 395 (Greig 148, Knott 87;
                    Julien 5 – 57)
                    2nd innings: 277 for 7 (Fletcher 129 not
                    out, Knott 67)
West Indies: 1st innings: 596 for 8 dec. (Rowe 302,
                    Kallicharran 119, Murray 53 not out;
                    Greig 6 – 164)

Fourth Test – Georgetown
MATCH DRAWN
England: 1st innings: 448 (Greig 121, Amiss 118,
                    Knott 61)
West Indies: 1st innings: 198 for 4 (Fredericks 98)

Fifth Test – Port of Spain
ENGLAND won by 26 runs
England:　　1st innings: 267 (Boycott 99)
　　　　　　2nd innings: 263 (Boycott 112)
West Indies: 1st innings: 305 (Rowe 123, Lloyd 52;
　　　　　　　Greig 8 – 86)
　　　　　　2nd innings: 199 (Greig 5 – 70)

TEST AVERAGES:

ENGLAND

Batting	I	NO	R	HS	Ave
D. L. Amiss	9	1	663	262*	82.87
A. W. Greig	9	0	430	148	47.77
G. Boycott	9	0	421	112	46.77
A. P. E. Knott	9	1	365	87	45.62
K. W. R. Fletcher	7	1	262	129*	43.66
M. H. Denness	9	0	231	67	25.66
R. D. G. Willis	5	4	25	10*	25.00
J. A. Jameson	4	0	73	38	18.25
D. L. Underwood	7	3	67	24	16.75
F. C. Hayes	7	0	60	24	8.57
G. G. Arnold	5	1	34	13	8.50
P. I. Pocock	7	0	52	23	7.42
C. M. Old	7	0	50	19	7.14
J. Birkenshaw	3	0	15	8	5.00

Bowling	O	M	R	W	Ave
J. A. Jameson	7	2	17	1	17.00
A. W. Greig	207.1	46	543	24	22.62
J. Birkenshaw	40	9	96	2	48.00
R. G. D. Willis	73	15	255	5	51.00
P. I. Pocock	200	50	550	9	61.11
C. M. Old	87.4	15	313	5	62.60
D. L. Underwood	137.5	45	314	5	62.80
G. G. Arnold	49.3	11	148	2	74.00
K. W. R. Fletcher	0.5	0	5	0	–

WEST INDIES

Batting	I	NO	R	HS	Ave
L. G. Rowe	7	0	616	302	88.00
R. C. Fredericks	7	1	397	98	66.16
A. I. Kallicharran	7	0	397	158	56.71
B. D. Julien	5	1	172	86*	43.00
D. L. Murray	5	2	113	53*	37.66
K. D. Boyce	4	1	87	34*	29.00
R. B. Kanhai	7	1	157	44	26.16
C. H. Lloyd	7	1	147	52	24.50
G. St. A. Sobers	5	5	100	57	20.00
Inshan Ali	3	0	29	15	9.66
V. A. Holder	1	0	8	8	8.00
L. R. Gibbs	4	2	9	6*	4.50
A. G. Barrett	1	0	0	0	0.00
A. M. E. Roberts	1	1	9	9*	–

M. L. C. Foster did not bat.

Bowling	O	M	R	W	Ave
B. D. Julien	174	50	378	16	23.62
C. H. Lloyd	56	21	71	3	23.66
K. D. Boyce	118.4	23	324	11	29.45
G. St. A. Sobers	223.2	92	421	14	30.07
L. R. Gibbs	328.3	103	661	18	36.72
A. G. Barrett	124	46	260	7	37.14
A. M. E. Roberts	50	12	124	3	41.33
Inshan Ali	113	34	248	5	49.60
V. A. Holder	42	12	105	2	52.50
R. C. Fredericks	34	7	93	1	93.00
M. L. C. Foster	16	5	32	0	–
L. G. Rowe	3	1	6	0	–
R. B. Kanhai	3	1	8	0	–
A. I. Kallicharran	4	0	17	0	–

WITH THE TOURISTS–IN ENGLAND IN 1974

INDIA

First Test – Old Trafford
ENGLAND won by 113 runs.
England : 1st innings : 328 for 9 dec. (Fletcher 123 not out, Amiss 56, Greig 53)

           2nd innings : 213 for 3 dec. (Edrich 100 not out)

India :   1st innings : 246 (Gavaskar 101, Abid Ali 71; Willis 4 – 64)

           2nd innings : 182 (Gavaskar 58, Viswanath 50; Old 4 – 20)

Second Test – Lords
ENGLAND won by innings and 285 runs.
England : 1st innings : 629 (Amiss 188, Denness 118, Greig 106; Bedi 6 – 226)

India :   1st innings : 302 (Engineer 86, Viswanath 52; Old 4 – 67)

           2nd innings : 42 (Old 5 – 21, Arnold 4– 19)

Third Test – Edgbaston
ENGLAND won by innings and 78 runs.
England : 1st innings : 459 for 2 dec. (D. Lloyd 214 not out, Denness 100, Amiss 79, Fletcher 51 not out)

India :   1st innings : 165 (Engineer 64 not out; Hendrick 4 – 28)

           2nd innings : 216 (Naik 77)

TEST AVERAGES:

ENGLAND

Batting	I	NO	R	HS	Ave
D. Lloyd	2	1	260	214*	260.00
K. W. R. Fletcher	3	2	189	123*	109.00
J. H. Edrich	3	1	203	100*	101.50
M. H. Denness	4	1	289	118	96.33
D. L. Amiss	4	0	370	188	92.50
A. W. Greig	2	0	159	106	79.50
R. G. D. Willis	1	0	24	24	24.00
A. P. E. Knott	2	0	26	26	13.00
D. L. Underwood	3	0	25	9	8.33
G. Boycott	2	0	16	10	8.00
C. M. Old	2	0	15	12	7.50
G. G. Arnold	1	0	5	5	5.00
M. Hendrick	1	1	1	1*	–

Bowling	O	M	R	W	Ave
C. M. Old	89	19	249	18	13.83
M. Hendrick	85	14	215	14	15.35
R. G. D. Willis	36	8	97	5	19.50
G. G. Arnold	65.5	13	204	10	20.40
A. W. Greig	70.1	16	176	6	29.33
D. L. Underwood	67	25	146	4	36.50
D. Lloyd	2	0	4	0	–

INDIA

Batting	I	NO	R	HS	Ave
S. S. Naik	2	0	81	77	40.50
F. M. Engineer	6	1	195	86	39.00
S. Gavaskar	6	0	217	101	36.16
G. R. Viswanath	6	0	200	52	33.33
A. V. Mankad	2	0	57	43	28.50
E. D. Solkar	6	1	98	43	19.60
S. Abid Ali	6	0	101	71	16.83
A. L. Wadekar	6	0	82	36	13.66
S. Venkataraghavan	4	1	13	5*	4.33
B. S. Bedi	6	1	15	14	3.00
S. Madan Lal	4	0	11	7	2.75
P. B. Patel	4	0	10	5	2.50
E. A. S. Prasanna	4	0	9	5	2.25
B. S. Chandrasekhar	3	2	2	2	2.00

Bowling	O	M	R	W	Ave
S. Abid Ali	81.3	12	252	6	42.00
B. S. Bedi	172.2	28	523	10	52.30
B. S. Chandrasekhar	42	7	126	2	63.00
E. A. S. Prasanna	86	10	267	3	89.00
S. Madan Lal	73	19	188	2	94.00
E. D. Solkar	44	11	125	1	125.00
S. Venkataraghavan	37	3	96	0	–

PAKISTAN

First Test – Headingley
MATCH DRAWN
Pakistan: 1st innings: 285 (Majid Khan 75, Sarfraz Nawaz 53)
2nd innings: 179
England: 1st innings: 183
2nd innings: 238 for 6 (Edrich 70, Fletcher 67 not out; Sarfraz Nawaz 4 – 56)

Second Test – Lords
MATCH DRAWN
Pakistan: 1st innings: 130 for 9 dec. (Underwood 5 – 20)
2nd innings: 226 (Mushtaq Mohammad 76, Wasim Raja 53; Underwood 8 – 51)
England: 1st innings: 270 (Knott 83)
2nd innings: 27 for 0

Third Test – Oval
MATCH DRAWN
Pakistan: 1st innings: 600 for 7 dec. (Zaheer Abbas 240, Majid Khan 98, Mushtaq Mohammad 76)
2nd innings: 94 for 4
England: 1st innings: 545 (Amiss 183, Fletcher 122, Old 65; Intikhab 5 – 116)

TEST AVERAGES:

ENGLAND

Batting	I	NO	R	HS	Ave
K. W. R. Fletcher	4	1	208	122	69.33
D. L. Amiss	5	1	220	183	55.00
C. M. Old	4	1	116	65	38.66
J. H. Edrich	4	0	144	70	36.00
A. P. E. Knott	4	0	132	83	33.00
D. L. Underwood	3	1	64	43	32.00
D. Lloyd	5	1	96	48	24.00
M. H. Denness	4	0	91	44	22.75
A. W. Greig	4	0	90	37	22.50
M. Hendrick	2	1	7	6	7.00
G. G. Arnold	3	0	13	10	4.33
R. G. D. Willis	1	1	1	1*	–

Bowling	O	M	R	W	Ave
D. L. Underwood	113.5	11	218	17	12.82
A. W. Greig	79.5	23	222	8	27.75
G. G. Arnold	121	28	300	10	30.00
M. Hendrick	68	16	195	6	32.50
C. M. Old	88.3	8	324	7	46.28
R. G. D. Willis	35	4	129	2	64.50
D. Lloyd	2	0	13	0	–

PAKISTAN

Batting	I	NO	R	HS	Ave
Zaheer Abbas	6	0	324	240	54.00
Wasim Raja	4	1	135	53	45.00
Majid Khan	6	0	262	98	43.66
Mushtaq Mohammad	6	0	209	76	34.83
Sadiq Mohammad	6	0	148	43	24.66
Sarfraz Nawaz	5	2	70	53	23.33
Imran Khan	6	1	92	31	18.40
Intikhab Alam	5	1	50	32*	12.50
Shafiq Ahmed	2	0	25	18	12.50
Asif Iqbal	5	0	53	29	10.60
Wasim Bari	4	0	10	4	2.50
Asif Masood	3	3	23	17*	–

Bowling	O	M	R	W	Ave
Sarfraz Nawaz	121	34	259	9	28.77
Intikhab Alam	98.4	25	235	8	29.37
Asif Masood	104	28	235	7	33.57
Asif Iqbal	16	4	34	1	34.00
Mushtaq Mohammad	41	17	75	2	37.50
Imran Khan	112	26	258	5	51.60
Wasim Raja	25	6	76	1	76.00
Majid Khan	2	0	10	0	–

TEST CRICKET: ENGLAND'S RECORD

V AUSTRALIA	WON BY England	Australia	Drawn
In Australia	43	59	17
In England	28	27	46
	—	—	—
	71	86	63

V SOUTH AFRICA	WON BY England	South Africa	Drawn
In South Africa	25	13	20
In England	21	5	18
	—	—	—
	46	18	38

V WEST INDIES	WON BY England	West Indies	Drawn
In West Indies	7	8	17
In England	12	11	8
	—	—	—
	19	19	25

V NEW ZEALAND	WON BY England	New Zealand	Drawn
In New Zealand	10	0	13
In England	13	0	11
	—	—	—
	23	0	24

V INDIA	WON BY England	India	Drawn
In India	4	5	14
In England	18	1	6
	—	—	—
	22	6	20

V PAKISTAN	WON BY England	Pakistan	Drawn
In Pakistan	1	0	8
In England	8	1	9
	—	—	—
	9	1	17

1974 FINAL COUNTY CHAMPIONSHIP TABLE

		Plyd	Won	Lost	Drawn	Tie	No Result	Bonus Pts. Btg.	Bwlg.	Total Pts.
1	Worcestershire	20	11	3	6	—	—	45	72	227
2	Hampshire	20	10	3	6	—	1	55	70	225
3	Northamptonshire	20	9	2	9	—	—	46	67	203
4	Leicestershire	20	7	7	6	—	—	47	69	186
5	Somerset	20	6	4	10	—	—	49	72	181
6	Middlesex	20	7	5	8	—	—	45	56	171
7	Surrey	20	6	4	10	—	—	42	69	171
8	Lancashire	20	5	0	15	—	—	47	66	163
9	Warwickshire	20	5	5	10	—	—	44	65	159
10	Kent	20	5	8	7	—	—	33	63	146
11	Yorkshire	20	4	7	8	—	1	37	69	146
12	Essex	20	4	3	12	1	—	45	51	141
13	Sussex	20	4	9	6	1	—	29	63	137
14	Gloucestershire	20	4	9	6	—	1	29	55	124
15	Nottinghamshire	20	1	9	10	—	—	42	66	118
16	Glamorgan	20	2	7	10	—	1	28	56	104
17	Derbyshire	20	1	6	13	—	—	23	62	95

1974 JOHN PLAYER SUNDAY LEAGUE FINAL TABLE

		Plyd	Won	Lost	Tie	No Result	Points
1	Leicestershire	16	12	1	1	2	54
2	Somerset	16	12	2	0	2	52
3	Kent	16	10	4	0	2	44
4	Northamptonshire	16	10	6	0	0	40
5	Hampshire	16	9	5	0	2	40
6	Sussex	16	8	6	1	1	36
7	Yorkshire	16	8	6	0	2	36
8	Middlesex	16	7	7	1	1	32
9	Worcestershire	16	7	7	0	2	32
10	Surrey	16	7	8	0	1	30
11	Warwickshire	16	7	8	0	1	30
12	Lancashire	16	5	9	1	1	24
13	Gloucestershire	16	4	8	0	4	24
14	Glamorgan	16	5	10	0	1	22
15	Essex	16	4	11	0	1	18
16	Derbyshire	16	4	11	0	1	18
17	Nottinghamshire	16	3	13	0	0	12

1974 GILLETTE CUP FINAL

Kent v Lancashire

Played at Lord's Monday, 9th September (after play on Saturday, 7th September had been postponed).

LANCASHIRE

D. Lloyd	c Woolmer b Graham	2
B. Wood	b Woolmer	17
H. Pilling	c Knott b Woolmer	9
C. H. Lloyd	run out	25
A. Kennedy	c Ealham b Johnson	9
F. M. Engineer	st Knott b Graham-Brown	15
D. P. Hughes	run out	15
J. Simmons	c Knott b Graham-Brown	3
K. Shuttleworth	run out	7
P. Lever	b Graham	3
P. Lee	not out	5
Extras (B 1, LB 4, W 2, NB 1)		8

Total (60 overs) 118

Fall of wickets: 1 for 10; 2 for 30; 3 for 37; 4 for 68; 5 for 72; 6 for 97; 7 for 98; 8 for 104; 9 for 111.

KENT

B. W. Luckhurst	b Lee	16
G. W. Johnson	b Wood	17
M. C. Cowdrey	b Simmons	7
M. H. Denness	b Wood	1
A. G. E. Ealham	b Lee	17
J. N. Shepherd	c and b Wood	19
A. P. E. Knott	not out	18
R. A. Woolmer	not out	15
Extras (B 3, LB 1, W 4, NB 4)		12

Total for 6 wickets (46.5 overs) 122

Did not bat: J. Graham-Brown, D. L. Underwood, J. N. Graham.
Fall of wickets: 1 for 37; 2 for 52; 3 for 52; 4 for 53; 5 for 75; 6 for 89.

BOWLING

Kent	O	M	R	W	Lancashire	O	M	R	W
Graham	11	6	14	2	Lever	12	3	39	0
Shepherd	9	2	16	0	Shuttleworth	1	0	3	0
Underwood	9	3	18	0	Lee	12	3	30	2
Woolmer	12	2	20	2	Simmons	6.5	3	14	1
Johnson	7	0	27	1	Wood	12	5	18	3
Graham-Brown	12	5	15	2	Hughes	3	0	6	0

KENT WON BY FOUR WICKETS

D

1974 BENSON & HEDGES CUP FINAL
Leicestershire v Surrey
Played at Lords 20th July.

SURREY

J. H. Edrich	c and b Steele	40
L. E. Skinner	lbw b Higgs	0
G. P. Howarth	c Tolchard b Booth	22
Younis Ahmed	c Dudleston b Illingworth	43
G. R. J. Roope	b McKenzie	13
S. J. Storey	lbw b Illingworth	2
R. D. Jackman	c Tolchard b McKenzie	36
A. R. Butcher	c Tolchard b Higgs	7
P. J. Pocock	b Higgs	0
A. Long	c Tolchard b Higgs	0
G. G. Arnold	not out	0
Extras (B 5, NB 2)		7

Total (54.1 overs) 170

Fall of wickets: 1 for 4; 2 for 36; 3 for 99; 4 for 111; 5 for 118; 6 for 137; 8 for 168; 9 for 168.

LEICESTERSHIRE

B. Dudleston	lbw b Arnold	0
J. F. Steele	run out	18
M. E. J. C. Norman	lbw b Roope	24
B. F. Davison	c Howarth b Arnold	13
R. W. Tolchard	lbw b Roope	0
J. C. Balderstone	b Pocock	32
R. Illingworth	b Arnold	23
N. M. McVicker	c Edrich b Pocock	10
G. D. McKenzie	st Long b Pocock	0
P. Booth	c Arnold b Jackman	5
K. Higgs	not out	8
Extras (B 1, LB 5, NB 4)		10

Total (54 overs) 143

Fall of wickets: 1 for 0; 2 for 46; 3 for 46; 4 for 50; 5 for 65; 6 for 113; 7 for 129; 8 for 129; 9 for 131.

BOWLING

Leicestershire	O	M	R	W	Surrey	O	M	R	W
McKenzie	10.1	0	31	2	Arnold	10	4	20	3
Higgs	7	2	10	4	Jackman	11	1	34	1
Booth	8	1	30	1	Roope	11	2	30	2
McVicker	8	1	25	0	Butcher	11	1	23	0
Illingworth	11	2	36	2	Pocock	11	1	26	3
Steele	10	0	31	1					

SURREY WON BY 27 RUNS

98

THE TOP TWENTY

– In all first-class 1974 season cricket (not one-day matches)

BATSMEN

	I	NO	R	HS	Ave
C. H. Lloyd (Lancs)	31	8	1458	178*	63.39
B. A. Richards (Hants)	27	4	1406	225*	61.13
G. M. Turner (Worcs)	31	9	1332	202*	60.55
G. Boycott (Yorks)	36	6	1783	160*	59.43
R. T. Virgin (Nhnts)	39	5	1936	144*	56.94
D. L. Amiss (Warw)	31	3	1510	155	53.93
J. H. Edrich (Surrey)	23	2	1126	152*	53.62
J. H. Hampshire (Yorks)	23	6	901	158	53.00
R. B. Kanhai (Warw)	22	4	936	213*	52.00
J. A. Jameson (Warw)	42	2	1932	240*	48.30
G. St. A. Sobers (Notts)	27	4	1110	132*	48.26
D. Lloyd (Lancs)	22	2	958	214*	47.90
B. F. Davison (Leics)	39	3	1670	142	46.38
Zaheer Abbas (Glos)	30	4	1182	240	45.46
Majid Khan (Glam)	35	3	1451	164	45.34
B. L. D'Oliveira (Worc)	26	3	1026	227	44.61
M. J. Harris (Notts)	41	3	1690	133	44.47
M. J. Smith (M'sex)	38	4	1468	170*	43.18
J. M. Brearley (M'sex)	36	5	1324	173*	42.70
Sadiq Mohammad (Glos)	32	2	1278	106	42.60

THE TOP TWENTY

– In all first-class 1974 season cricket (not one-day matches)

BOWLERS

	O	M	R	W	Ave
A. M. E. ROBERTS (Hants)	727.4	198	1621	119	13.62
G. G. Arnold (Surrey)	487	139	1069	75	14.25
V. A. Holder (Worcs)	659	146	1493	94	15.88
M. J. Procter (Glos)	311.3	80	776	47	16.51
B. L. D'Oliveira (Worcs)	345.3	105	697	40	17.42
M. N. S. Taylor (Hants)	541	147	1259	72	17.48
H. R. Moseley (Somerset)	661.5	198	1420	81	17.53
R. Illingworth (Leics)	535.1	204	1014	57	17.78
P. Carrick (Yorks)	405.4	167	840	47	17.87
S. Turner (Essex)	615.5	166	1317	73	18.04
S. J. Rouse (Warwicks)	164.5	34	489	23	18.11
D. L. Underwood (Kent)	563	228	1181	65	18.16
R. P. Baker (Surrey)	207.1	48	494	27	18.30
J. C. Balderstone (Leics)	134.4	33	351	19	18.47
G. D. McKenzie (Leics)	531.3	131	1345	71	18.94
C. M. Old (Yorks)	526.3	132	1366	72	18.97
R. A. Woolmer (Kent)	466.4	135	1065	56	19.01
N. Gifford (Worcs)	617	197	1333	69	19.32
R. S. Herman (Hants)	657.3	202	1426	73	19.53
R. M. H. Cottam (Nhnts)	454	133	1101	56	19.66

FOR THE COUNTIES

Their top six batsmen and bowlers in the
1974 County Championship

DERBYSHIRE

Batting

	M	I	NO	R	HS	Ave
L. G. Rowe	16	28	1	1000	94	37.04
A. Hill	8	16	3	398	140*	30.61
A. J. Harvey-Walker	17	29	1	727	117	25.96
J. B. Bolus	20	35	5	736	93	24.53
F. W. Swarbrook	18	30	10	466	65	23.30
A. Morris	3	6	1	113	37	22.60

Bowling

	O	M	R	W	Ave
M. Hendrick	278.3	72	637	34	18.74
G. Miller	329	77	883	40	22.07
A Ward	357.4	72	1092	48	22.75
S. Venkataraghavan	311.2	61	953	31	30.74
P. E. Russell	498.3	134	1237	38	32.55
K. Stevenson	147.2	12	586	16	36.63

ESSEX

Batting

	M	I	NO	R	HS	Ave
B. R. Hardie	20	34	2	1062	133	33.13
S. Turner	20	30	4	851	118*	32.73
K. S. McEwan	20	34	2	999	126	31.22
G. A. Gooch	15	25	3	637	114*	28.95
R. M. O. Cooke	17	27	4	641	100	27.87
B. E. A. Edmeades	18	31	1	650	54*	21.66

Bowling

	O	M	R	W	Ave
S. Turner	574.5	154	1228	68	18.05
K. D. Boyce	313.4	55	868	35	24.80
R. E. East	498.1	133	1241	45	27.57
K. R. Pont	81	20	194	7	27.71
R. N. S. Hobbs	325.1	87	907	32	28.34
B. E. A. Edmeades	157.4	34	375	13	28.84

GLAMORGAN

Batting	M	I	NO	R	HS	Ave
Majid Khan	6	12	0	451	164	37.58
L. W. Hill	14	24	4	718	96*	35.90
A Jones	19	34	1	1104	113	33.45
R. C. Davis	18	32	3	706	73	24.34
J. W. Solanky	15	25	5	452	71	22.60
G. P. Ellis	9	16	2	290	116	20.71

Bowling	O	M	R	W	Ave
M. A. Nash	539.5	124	1463	63	23.22
D. L. Williams	496	90	1542	53	29.09
A. E. Cordle	272.3	39	869	29	29.97
J. W. Solanky	290	59	880	24	36.66
R. C. Davis	432.5	135	919	22	41.77
B. J. Lloyd	50.2	11	175	4	43.75

GLOUCESTERSHIRE

Batting	M	I	NO	R	HS	Ave
R. D. V. Knight	19	33	5	1196	144	42.71
M. J. Procter	17	30	2	950	157	33.93
Sadiq Mohammad	4	7	0	237	88	33.85
D. R. Shepherd	17	27	0	674	101	24.96
R. B. Nicholls	12	21	2	436	68	22.95
C. A. Milton	11	18	1	390	76	22.94

Bowling	O	M	R	W	Ave
M. J. Procter	263.1	62	670	39	17.18
D. A. Graveney	307.3	79	848	39	21.74
A. Brown	302.4	69	823	30	27.43
J. Davey	261	46	730	25	29.20
R. D. V. Knight	303.3	68	894	25	35.76
J. B. Mortimore	487.4	108	1307	29	45.07

HAMPSHIRE

Batting

	M	I	NO	R	HS	Ave
B. A. Richards	16	23	4	1059	225*	55.73
R. M. C. Gilliat	19	26	2	882	106	36.75
D. R. Turner	19	26	1	898	152	35.92
P. J. Sainsbury	19	24	7	535	98	31.47
C. G. Greenidge	19	28	1	700	120	25.93
M. N. S. Taylor	19	22	2	437	68	21.85

Bowling

	O	M	R	W	Ave
A. M. E. Roberts	658.4	178	1493	111	13.45
R. R. Herman	574.3	181	1218	70	17.40
M. N. S. Taylor	472.2	126	1101	63	17.47
P. J. Sainsbury	376.2	185	651	33	19.72
N. G. Cowley	71	31	148	6	24.66
T. E. Jesty	270.1	78	620	22	28.18

KENT

Batting

	M	I	NO	R	HS	Ave
B. W. Luckhurst	20	32	2	1035	148	34.50
M. C. Cowdrey	19	27	3	801	122	33.37
C. J. C. Rowe	12	13	6	220	58*	31.42
G. W. Johnson	20	32	2	903	158	30.10
R. A. Woolmer	20	29	3	713	112	27.42
J. N. Shepherd	18	25	5	513	79	25.65

Bowling

	O	M	R	W	Ave
D. L. Underwood	319.1	139	645	40	16.12
R. A. Woolmer	424.4	121	981	54	18.16
B. D. Julien	93	21	266	12	22.16
G. W. Johnson	405.2	124	1025	36	28.47
J. N. Graham	400.4	89	971	34	28.55
B. W. Luckhurst	23	9	60	2	30.00

LANCASHIRE

Batting

	M	I	NO	R	HS	Ave
C. H. Lloyd	19	30	8	1403	178*	63.77
D. Lloyd	7	11	0	425	186	38.63
B. W. Reidy	3	4	1	112	69	37.33
H. Pilling	15	22	4	656	144	36.44
K. L. Snellgrove	10	15	4	395	75*	35.90
F. C. Hayes	20	31	1	1033	107	34.43

Bowling

	O	M	R	W	Ave
D. Lloyd	41	15	88	6	14.66
B. Wood	391.4	134	845	43	19.65
K. Shuttleworth	483.1	146	1168	50	23.36
C. H. Lloyd	22	8	47	2	23.50
P. Lever	485.1	128	1218	50	24.36
J. Simmons	572.1	175	1347	55	24.49

LEICESTERSHIRE

Batting

	M	I	NO	R	HS	Ave
B. F. Davison	20	32	2	1392	142	46.40
J. C. Balderstone	12	19	2	688	140	40.47
B. Dudleston	20	34	4	1059	135	35.30
R. W. Tolchard	20	30	7	546	103	23.73
N. M. McVicker	20	23	5	404	64	22.44
J. F. Steele	20	34	4	669	116*	22.30

Bowling

	O	M	R	W	Ave
J. C. Balderstone	111.3	27	284	18	15.77
R. Illingworth	484.3	172	972	53	18.33
G. D. McKenzie	440.5	98	1161	57	20.36
J. Birkenshaw	406.2	104	1004	42	23.90
N. M. McVicker	383.1	72	1090	43	25.34
P. Booth	86.5	12	270	10	27.00

MIDDLESEX

Batting

	M	I	NO	R	HS	Ave
J. M. Brearley	20	34	5	1292	173*	44.55
M. J. Smith	17	30	4	1107	170*	42.57
C. T. Radley	20	33	5	1004	111*	35.85
N. G. Featherstone	20	32	3	891	125	30.72
G. D. Barlow	11	19	2	446	70	26.23
J. T. Murray	20	27	3	584	82*	24.33

Bowling

	O	M	R	W	Ave
J. S. E. Price	153	33	451	21	21.47
F. J. Titmus	895.2	301	1837	85	21.61
D. A. Marriott	38	9	91	4	22.75
P. H. Edmonds	731.5	245	1628	71	22.92
N. G. Featherstone	42.5	9	132	5	26.40
M. J. Vernon	143	19	505	19	26.57

NORTHAMPTONSHIRE

Batting

	M	I	NO	R	HS	Ave
R. T. Virgin	20	36	5	1845	144*	59.22
P. J. Watts	19	32	7	995	104*	39.80
D. S. Steele	19	35	3	1004	104	31.37
Sarfraz Nawaz	5	8	3	132	38	26.40
A. Tait	14	24	0	540	99	22.50
P. Willey	20	34	3	678	100*	21.87

Bowling

	O	M	R	W	Ave
B. S. Bedi	456.3	15	997	55	18.12
A. Hodgson	222.8	51	561	29	19.34
R. M. H. Cottam	454	113	1101	56	19.66
J. C. J. Dye	492.1	98	1359	67	20.28
Sarfraz Nawaz	197.2	54	512	24	21.33
J. Swinburne	80	20	219	10	21.90

NOTTINGHAMSHIRE

Batting

	M	I	NO	R	HS	Ave
G. St. A. Sobers	15	27	4	1110	132*	48.26
M. J. Harris	19	35	3	1431	133	44.71
M. J. Smedley	20	36	6	1059	118*	35.30
H. T. Tunnicliffe	9	15	3	331	87	27.58
B. Hassan	18	35	4	770	78	24.84
D. W. Randall	18	34	4	639	81	21.30

Bowling

	O	M	R	W	Ave
R. A. White	667	186	1757	73	24.07
W. Taylor	218.4	38	636	24	26.50
H. T. Tunnicliffe	51	9	168	6	28.00
B. Stead	541	124	1493	52	28.71
H. C. Latchman	315.3	54	1067	37	28.84
G. St. A. Sobers	350.4	79	925	29	34.48

SOMERSET

Batting

	M	I	NO	R	HS	Ave
M. J. Kitchen	12	22	2	790	88	39.50
D. B. Close	20	34	7	984	114*	36.44
V. A. Richards	20	34	1	1154	107	34.97
D. Breakwell	16	24	7	552	67	32.47
D. J. S. Taylor	20	37	5	927	179	28.97
J. M. Parks	19	31	3	608	66	21.71

Bowling

	O	M	R	W	Ave
H. R. Moseley	567.5	169	1236	65	19.01
D. B. Close	95	30	249	13	19.15
B. A. Langford	412.1	153	937	42	22.31
A. A. Jones	528	113	1448	64	22.63
T. W. Cartwright	197	97	340	15	22.66
I. T. Botham	278.3	70	680	27	25.19

SURREY

Batting

	M	I	NO	R	HS	Ave
J. H. Edrich	9	14	1	578	152*	44.46
S. J. Storey	17	23	4	744	111	39.16
G. R. J. Roope	20	31	6	831	119	33.24
Younis Ahmed	19	33	4	907	116	31.28
G. P. Howarth	16	28	2	747	98	28.73
R. D. Jackman	18	23	4	469	92*	24.68

Bowling

	O	M	R	W	Ave
G. G. Arnold	275.1	92	515	51	10.09
R. P. Baker	190.1	43	459	25	18.36
R. D. Jackman	614.1	136	1581	79	20.01
S. J. Storey	180	48	401	16	25.06
P. I. Pocock	628.5	189	1511	60	25.18
A. R. Butcher	182	42	460	18	25.55

SUSSEX

Batting

	M	I	NO	R	HS	Ave
P. J. Graves	20	37	6	1224	145*	39.48
G. A. Greenidge	19	38	3	1041	147	29.74
M. G. Griffith	10	19	2	406	121*	23.88
M. J. J. Faber	13	24	2	492	112*	22.36
A. W. Greig	9	17	0	337	70	19.82
J. D. Morley	20	39	1	708	82*	18.63

Bowling

	O	M	R	W	Ave
J. A. Snow	508.1	107	1342	70	19.17
J. Spencer	440.3	108	1142	47	24.30
M. A. Buss	341	119	785	30	26.16
A. W. Greig	313.5	64	994	32	31.06
U. C. Joshi	182	54	431	13	33.15
C. P. Phillipson	137	29	355	10	35.50

WARWICKSHIRE

Batting

	M	I	NO	R	HS	Ave
D. L. Amiss	8	15	2	620	195	47.69
R. B. Kanhai	13	21	4	757	213*	44.52
J. A. Jameson	20	36	2	1420	240*	41.76
M. J. K. Smith	18	34	7	990	105	36.66
A. Kallicharran	20	34	2	1040	127	32.50
R. G. D. Willis	13	18	13	122	23*	24.40

Bowling

	O	M	R	W	Ave
S. J. Rouse	164.5	34	489	27	18.11
E. E. Hemmings	682	198	1709	82	20.84
R. G. D. Willis	313	54	949	44	21.56
D. J. Brown	431	105	1035	44	23.52
W. A. Bourne	135	26	431	13	33.15
W. Blenkiron	160.4	34	473	14	33.78

WORCESTERSHIRE

Batting

	M	I	NO	R	HS	Ave
G. M. Turner	18	28	8	1098	181	54.90
B. L. D'Oliveira	17	24	2	874	227	39.73
R. G. A. Headley	18	29	2	1018	137	37.70
T. J. Yardley	19	27	7	567	66*	28.35
J. M. Parker	15	23	1	608	140	27.64
E. J. O. Hemsley	8	12	0	301	85	25.08

Bowling

	O	M	R	W	Ave
V. A. Holder	600	131	1358	87	15.60
B. L. D'Oliveira	345.3	105	697	40	17.42
N. Gifford	573	185	1215	66	18.40
B. M. Brain	563.5	109	1576	75	21.01
J. D. Inchmore	213.5	37	680	28	24.28
J. Cumbes	180.5	33	482	18	26.77

YORKSHIRE

Batting	M	I	NO	R	HS	Ave
G. Boycott	15	26	5	1220	149*	58.10
J. H. Hampshire	13	22	6	879	158	54.94
R. G. Lumb	15	26	2	705	123*	29.38
B. Leadbeater	17	28	3	692	99*	27.68
P. Carrick	9	11	3	179	46	22.37
R. A. Hutton	14	22	4	337	102*	21.06

Bowling	O	M	R	W	Ave
C. M. Old	246	71	567	33	17.18
S. Oldham	20.5	5	69	4	17.25
P. Carrick	322.4	123	744	39	19.07
A. L. Robinson	320	78	798	34	23.47
G. A. Cope	620.4	198	1498	62	24.16
A. G. Nicholson	471	152	1100	44	25.00

ANSWERS

1. A. (a) Glamorgan (b) Blue and gold (c) Gold daffodil.
B. (a) Surrey (b) Chocolate (c) Prince of Wales'
Feathers.

2. 1. An over in which no runs are scored off the bowler.
2. An over in which no runs are scored but the bowler
captures at least one wicket. 3. 'Mr' Extras – runs not
coming from the bat (see answer to question 8 also).
4. The failure by a batsman to score a single run.
5. & 6. The 'on' and 'off' sides are determined by the
batsman taking strike. The 'on' side is the side in
which his legs are positioned. (It is often referred to
as the *leg-side*). The 'off' side is, of course, the side
further from his legs. The natural tendency is thus for
batsmen to hook and pull the ball to the on-side. To
cut, squarely or finely, to the off-side. (But, of course,
what has been the 'on' side to a right-handed batsman becomes the 'off' side to a left-handed one. Hence
the adjustment of fielding positions when a right-
hander gives strike to a left-hander.) 7. An individual
score of a hundred runs. 8. 2 Byes, 4 Leg byes, 2
Wides, 1 No Ball. 9. Being dismissed in both innings
of a match without scoring. Two 'ducks' would also
describe a 'pair of spectacles'. 10. In three-day county
cricket and five-day Test matches, most captains are
reluctant to send in to bat one of their recognised
batsmen when a wicket falls with only twenty minutes
or so left to be played before the close for the day.
Instead they would send in a lower-order batsman to
play out time – as a 'nightwatchman' keeping possession. There have been many instances when the 'nightwatchman' has in fact not only played out time on the
day but continued his innings for much of the next
day.

3. 1. (a) Marylebone Cricket Club (b) Melbourne Cricket Club. 2. Michael Colin Cowdrey. 3. Three. 4. Five. 5. 60. 6. 40. 7. 60 8. (a) 100 overs (b) 100 overs plus any overs less than a hundred needed to have bowled out their opponents e.g. if the side batting first were dismissed in 90 overs; their opponents had a maximum of 100 plus 10 overs in which to bat. 9. Mike Denness. 10. Ray Illingworth.

4. 1. Keith Fletcher (123 not out of 328 for 9 declared). 2. S. M. Gavaskar (101 run out). 3. John Edrich. 4. Chris Old. 5. David Lloyd of Lancashire. 6. Dennis Amiss (188), Mike Denness (118) and Tony Greig 106. 7. Chris Old 5 for 21 and Geoff Arnold 4 for 19. 8. (a) Old Trafford, Manchester. (b) Lord's, London and (c) Edgbaston, Birmingham. 9. David Lloyd. 10 A fast, rising ball from Old forced Mankad to make a sudden defensive stroke with his bat held high. The impact shook off his cap that fell on his stumps and dislodged a bail.

5. To crack the code, take the letter opposite the black square in the first column, then the letter opposite the black square in the second column, then the letters in the third, fourth, fifth, etc. columns, and so on, to find the names of Clive Lloyd of the West Indies and Lancashire, and Majid Khan of Pakistan and Glamorganshire.

6. 1. B. J. T. Bosanquet. 2. L. E. G. Ames. 3. P. G. H. Fender. 4. D. V. P. Wright. 5. C. W. L. Parker. 6. A. P. F. Chapman. J. W. H. T. Douglas was known as 'Johnny Won't Hit To-Day' because of his slow rate of scoring (by comparison with scoring rates generally at the time when he was playing).

7. 1. A. G. Barrett. 2. Clive Lloyd of Lancashire. 3. India – the players were N. J. Contractor and F. M. Engineer. 4. Bob Herman. 5. Gary Sobers. 6. Barry Richards. 7. John Jameson. 8. Yorkshire. 9. Sarfraz Nawaz. 10. Chris Balderstone.

8. The six players are Knott, Greig, Old, Arnold, Edrich and Amiss.

9. W. G. Grace.

10. 1. (a) Kent (b) Sussex (c) Surrey (d) Hampshire. 2. Alfred Mynn. 3. Felix. 4. Edward.

11. A. (a) Yorkshire (b) Oxford Blue, Cambridge Blue and Gold (c) White Rose of Yorkshire. B. (a) Nottinghamshire (b) Green and gold (c) County Badge of Nottinghamshire. C. (a) Essex (b) Blue, gold and red (c) Three scimitars. The word 'ESSEX' is also included underneath, but was marked out for the purpose of this puzzle.

12. 1. Derbyshire, Gloucestershire, Kent, Lancashire, Middlesex, Nottinghamshire, Surrey, Sussex and Yorkshire. 2. Essex, Leicestershire, Warwickshire. 3. Worcestershire in 1899 and Northamptonshire in 1905. 4. Glamorgan. 5. Sussex. 6. Wilfred Rhodes (763 appearances) for Yorkshire and Frank Woolley (707 appearances) for Kent.

13. 1. B. Luckhurst. 2. G. D. McKenzie. 3. S. Turner. 4. J. M. Brearley. 5. A. Roberts. 6. V. A. Richards. 7. M. Hendrick. 8. Younis Ahmed. 9. G. M. Turner. 10. R. A. White.

14. The names of the fielding positions have been inserted for you. You may notice that because the bowler is swinging the ball away from the batsman's leg-side towards the off, it is on the off-side that most fielders have been placed. (See also answer to Puzzle 24.)

15. 1. d. 2. 1st – d, 2nd – b, 3rd – c, 4th – a. 3. c. 4. Four. 5. 1st – b, 2nd – d, 3rd – a, 4th – c. 6. Gary Sobers. 7. 1st – c, 2nd – b, 3rd – a. 8. a. 9. 1st – b, 2nd – a, 3rd –c, 4th – d. 10. c.

16. 1. Surrey by 27 runs. 2. John Edrich (Surrey), Ray Illingworth (Leics). 3. Kent by 4 wickets. 4. (a) Alan Knott. (b) Faroukh Engineer. 5. Roger Tolchard. 6. Ken Higgs. 7. Graham McKenzie. 8. The rule that members of an overseas touring team cannot take part in a county match during the period of a tour prevented the two Pakistani players, Intikhab Alam and Asif Iqbal, playing for Surrey and Kent respectively. 9. Clive Lloyd of Lancashire – 25 runs. 10. (a) John Edrich (Surrey) (b) Alan Knott (Kent).

17. Don Bradman.

18. A. (a) Northamptonshire (b) Maroon (c) Tudor Rose.
B. (a) Sussex (b) Dark blue, light blue and gold (c)
County Arms of Six Martlets. C. (a) Leicestershire
(b) Scarlet and dark green (c) Running fox in gold
on a green background.

19. 1. England C & D. 2. Australia B & C. 3. New Zealand B & C. 4. West Indies B & C. 5. England A & B.
6. England B & C. 7. Australia C & D. 8. England C.
9. India B & C. 10. Pakistan C & D. 11. South Africa
B & C. 12. Australia B. 13. West Indies C & D. 14.
South Africa A & B. 15. Australia A.

20. 1. Kingston, Jamaica. 2. Lahore, Pakistan. 3. Johannesburg, S. Africa. 4. Auckland, New Zealand. 5.
Calcutta, India. 6. Brisbane, Queensland, Australia.
7. Trinidad, West Indies. 8. Christchurch, New Zealand. 9. Cape Town, South Africa. 10. Barbados, West
Indies.

21. 1. Carrick. 2. Procter. 3. Grieves. 4. Boycott. 5.
Brookes. 6. Cowdrey. 7. Gilliat.

22. A. Walters. B. Chappell. C. Lillee. D. Mallett. E.
Thomson. F. Redpath. G. Walker. H. Marsh. A4 T,
B2 H, C6 E, D2 A, E5 S, F7 H, G5 E, H4 S, making
THE ASHES.

23. 1. Mike Hendrick. 2. Fred Trueman. 3. Peter Sainsbury. 4. Bob Woolmer. 5. Clive Radley. 6. Bob Cot-
tam. 7. Gary Sobers. 8. Tom Cartwright. 9. Geoff
Arnold. 10. Norman Gifford.

24. Differences in fielding positions from Puzzle 14 (the outswinging bowler): – Positions, of course, are not fixed, as captains (usually in consultation with the bowler) alter them to suit conditions, such as the state of the pitch, the situation in a match and the strengths and the weaknesses of the particular batsmen at the wicket. However, as compared with the basic setting for the outswinging bowler (Puzzle 14), the differences would generally be that one of the three slips would have come across to leg slip. A fine leg would have been introduced instead of third man. Mid-on, widish for the outswinger, would have come closer to the bowler's wicket and a little deeper; mid-off would have moved wider away from the wicket; gully, cover and short-leg would stay more or less the same. The reason is that the inswinging ball is moving *towards* the batsman and catches and shots would be more frequent on the leg, or on-, side.

25. 1. M. Nash. 2. R. D. V. Knight. 3. J. A. Snow. 4. R. T. Virgin. 5. J. A. Jameson. 6. C. H. Lloyd. 7. B. A. Richards. 8. J. S. E. Price. 9. B. R. Hardie. 10. C. M. Old.

26. 1. Engineer is an Indian, the other four West Indians. 2. Trevor Jesty bats and bowls right-handed, the others are right-hand batsmen but left-hand bowlers. 3. Fred Titmus is an off-break bowler, the others are fast bowlers. 4. Barry Wood – the others are wicket-keepers. 5. Clive Radley – the others were all 'Blues' for Oxford or Cambridge. 6. Bishen Bedi plays for India, the others for Pakistan. 7. Brian Davison was born in Rhodesia, the others were all born in South Africa. 8. Roger Prideaux – the others have all played football as professionals in the Football League. 9. Geoff Boycott – the other batsmen all played against Australia on M.C.C.'s 1974-5 tour. 10. Dennis Amiss (born Birmingham), the others were all born in India.

27. Jack Hobbs.

28. 1. Derbyshire. 2. Essex. 3. Glamorganshire. 4. Gloucestershire. 5. Hampshire. 6. Kent. 7. Lancashire 8. Leicestershire. 9. Middlesex. 10. Northamptonshire. 11. Nottinghamshire. 12. Somerset. 13. Surrey. 15. Warwickshire. 16. Worcestershire. 17. Yorkshire.

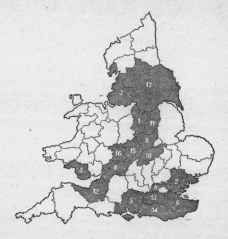

30. 1. F. R. Spofforth at Melbourne 1878–79. 2. W. Bates, also at Melbourne 1882–83. 3. C. Bannerman 165 not out in the very first Test match played – at Melbourne 1876–77. 4. W. G. Grace 152 in the first Test played in England – at the Oval in 1880.   5. E. D. Weekes: 141 v England in 1947–48 and then against India in 1948–49 he scored consecutively 128, 194, 162 and 101. 6. C. L. Walcott in the 1954–55 series against Australia scored 108, 126 and 110, 155 and 110. 7. 45 against Australia at Sydney 1886–87. 8. 36 against England at Birmingham in 1902. 9. T. G. Evans (England) 219 in 91 matches, with 173 caught and 46 stumped. 10. F. S. Trueman 307 in 67 matches.

31. 1. Compton. 2. Alec and Eric Bedser. 3. John for Leicestershire and David for Northamptonshire. 4. Greg and Ian Chappell. Ian is the captain. 5. Langridge. 6. Buss. 7. Dayle Robert and Richard John. 8. (a) Somerset and Hampshire (b) Somerset. 9. (a) Leicestershire (b) Jeffrey Graham and Roger William (c) Roger.

32. 1. 1877. 2. At the Oval in 1882 Australia defeated England by seven runs – their first victory in a Test in England (they had only played one earlier match, in 1880). The following day an 'obituary notice' was published in the *Sporting Times* that made reference to 'the ashes' of English cricket. Later that year the English team toured Australia. Australia won the First Test but after England had won the Second and Third Test matches some Australian ladies presented the Hon. Ivo Bligh, the England captain, with a small urn containing the ashes of a burnt stump. Although Australia halved the series by winning the Fourth Test of that series in which only four matches were played, England were left as the first holders of the Ashes! The story appealed to cricket lovers at the time and the term 'the Ashes' has remained signifying the special link between England and Australia in the world of cricket, with one country said to be holding the Ashes until the other, as the clear winner in a Test series, regains possession. 3. Only once – Australia in 1920–21. 4. When they won the first two of three Test matches played in England's 1891–92 tour of Australia. 5. W. M. Woodfull. 6. Len Hutton. 7. (a) Richie Benaud (b) C. C. McDonald 65.00. 8. R. Benaud (b) R. B. Simpson (c) W. M. Lawry (d) E. R. Dexter (e) M. J. K. Smith. 9. Ray Illingworth.

33. A. (a) Lancashire (b) Red, green and blue (c) Red Rose. B. (a) Worcestershire (b) Dark green and black (c) Shield, *Argent* bearing *Fess* between three *Pears Sable*. C. (a) Warwickshire (b) Blue, yellow and white (c) Bear and ragged staff.

34. 1. Ian Redpath (Victoria). 2. 'The General' Mc-Cosker (New South Wales). 3. Ian Chappell (South Australia). 4. Ross Edwards (Western Australia). 5. Greg Chappell (Queensland). 6. Rodney Marsh (Western Australia). 7. A. A. Mallett (South Australia). 8. K. J. O'Keefe (New South Wales). 9. Geoff Dymock (Queensland). 10. Max Walker (Victoria). 11 Jeff Thomson (Queensland). 12. Wally Edwards (Western Australia). (McCosker's nickname, incidentally, comes from the Australians' feeling that his name sounds a bit like that of the American General Custer! You will appreciate that, in a cricket context, there are many jokes based upon Custer's Last Stand! Mc-Cosker's *first* stand in a Test match against England in 1975 was to share in a partnership of 96 runs with Ian Redpath. McCosker himself going on to score 80 runs.)

35. 1. Yorkshire – all were regular openers for England. 2. Kent – all were England captains in Test matches.

3. Kent – all kept wicket for England. 4. Surrey – all opened the innings for England. 5. Middlesex – all were Nos. 3 and/or 4 batsmen for England against the Australians. 6. Surrey – all kept wicket for England. 7. Surrey – all were fast bowlers for England. 8. Nottinghamshire – all captained England against Australia. 9. Lancashire – all made centuries against the Australians in Test matches. 10. Sussex – all captained England in Test matches.

36. 1. (a) Yorkshire (b) Surrey (c) Nottinghamshire. 2. Glamorgan and Hampshire. 3. Derbyshire. 4. Essex, Leicestershire, Northamptonshire, Somerset, Sussex. 5. Nottinghamshire – on five occasions. 6. Surrey – 8 times. 7. Surrey – from 1952 to 1958 inclusive. 8. (a) Middlesex (b) Surrey (c) Hampshire. 9. (a) Middlesex (b) Gloucestershire (c) Northamptonshire.

37. Worcester(shire) who won the County Championship and Leicester(shire) who won the John Player League.

38. Len Hutton.

39. 1. Chris Balderstone. 2. Brian Close. 3. Barry Wood. 4. Jack Birkenshaw. 5. Barry Stead. 6. Mike Smedley. All were born in Yorkshire. The first five all played County cricket for Yorkshire before moving elsewhere. Mike Smedley played for Yorkshire's 2nd XI.

40. 1. Surrey. 2. Australia. 3. Surrey. 4. Northamptonshire. 5. West Indies. 6. Hampshire (he was, in fact, a grandson of the poet). 7. South Africa. 8. Surrey. 9. Yorkshire. 10. South Africa.

41. The essential difference between limited-over and other cricket is that there is no requirement for one side to dismiss all their opponent's batsmen to win a match in limited-over cricket. All that matters is the number of runs scored. If one side has scored 150 runs and lost all their wickets in doing so, they would still beat a side who had scored 149 runs without losing a wicket in the number of overs allowed by the competition. The first consideration in limited-over cricket is to keep down the number of runs scored. The first consideration in Championship cricket would normally be to capture wickets. So in the field-setting below, the captain has not, as he did in Puzzle 14, used three fielders in the slips in the hope of catching out the batsman. He has set his field to limit the number of runs.

42. 1. Gilbert Jessop. 2. P. G. H. Fender. 3. C. G. Macartney. 4. J. M. Gregory. 5. J. A. Jameson 240 and R. B. Kanhai 213 both not out. 6. Harry Pilling 144 (career best) and Clive Lloyd 178 not out. 7. Gordon Greenidge. 8. Gary Sobers. 9. Barry Richards.

43. A. (a) Hampshire (b) Blue, gold and white (c) Tudor rose and crown. B. (a) Gloucestershire (b) Blue, gold, brown, sky-blue, green and red (c) Coat of Arms of the City and County of Bristol. C. (a) Kent (b) Red and white (c) White horse.

44. 1. Paper A is correct. 2. Paper A is correct. 3. Paper B is correct. 4. Paper B is correct. 5. If it was correct that Smedley's highest score was 18 not out, and even allowing that he scored 18 on each of the six times he was not out, the number of runs he scored in his 30 completed innings must have been 1059 minus 108 (from the 'not out' innings). But the average of 951 runs from 30 completed innings would be more than his highest score! The highest score of 18 not out should have read 118 not out. 6. If Gifford bowled 185 maiden overs he must have bowled more than the printed number of 57.3 overs. The number of overs bowled was actually 573.

45. A. D. L. Amiss. B. J. D. Bond. C. J. Cumbes. D. M. H. Denness. E. P. H. Edmonds. F. M. J. J. Faber. G. C. G. (Gordon) Greenidge or G. A. (Geoff) Greenidge. H. J. H. Hampshire. I. R. Illingworth. J. R. D. Jackman. K. Majid Khan. L. P. Lever. M. J. T. Murray. N. A. G. (Tony) Nicholson. O. C. M. Old. P. J. M. Parks. Q. W. G. Quaife. R. A. M. E. Roberts. S. J. W. Solanky. T. G. M. Turner. U. D. L. Underwood. V. R. T. Virgin. W. R. G. D. Willis. Y. Younis (Ahmed). Z. Zaheer (Abbas).

46. 1. G. S. Sobers. 2. A. Jones. 3. R. D. Jackman. 4. B. F. Davison. 5. R. A. Woolmer. 6. M. J. Procter. 7. P. J. Graves. 8. H. R. Moseley. 9. E. E. Hemmings. 10. Bishen Bedi.

47. 1. India C & D. 2. Australia C. 3. West Indies C & D. 4. Australia B. 5. Australia B. 6. Pakistan C. 7. New Zealand C. 8. Australia B & C. 9. West Indies C. 10. England A & B. 11. Pakistan D. 12. England C & D. 13. South Africa C. 14. England C. 15. England B.

48. Wally Hammond.

49. 1. True. 2. True. 3. False – Cambridgeshire competed between 1864–9 and again in 1871. 4. True. 5. False – Phil Mead holds the record with 132 centuries. 6. True. 7. True. 8. False – John Edrich had 67 caps to Alan Knott's 66. 9. False – he made his first Test appearance in March 1974 before the County Championship season began. 10. False – Sussex beat Worcestershire in the first Final by 14 runs.

50. 1. b. 2. Lancashire in 1970, 1971 and 1972. 3. 1969. 4. Lancashire in 1969 and 1970; Kent in 1972 and 1973. 5. 1972. 6. Leicestershire. 7. (a) Somerset (b) Kent (c) Lancashire (d) Worcestershire. 8. P. W. Denning 112 runs for Somerset, and B. Luckhurst 125 runs for Kent. 9. (a) Leicestershire (b) Somerset (c) Lancashire (d) Surrey. 10. Brian Luckhurst again – 111 runs.

51. Because this is a limited-over field the changes between the setting for a fast and a slow bowler are usually fewer than they would be in a Championship match. The players set to limit the number of *single* runs have stayed more or less in the same places – third man, cover, deep cover, backward point, and

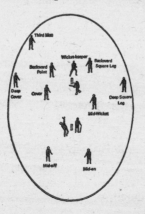

mid-wicket for example. The wicket-keeper, looking for a stumping, can stay closer to the stumps but the main changes are that square leg has moved to backward square leg and fine leg comes round to deep square leg, whilst both mid-on and mid-off (partly because the slow bowler can be expected to field more off his own bowling than could the fast bowler) have moved deeper.

52. 1. B. J. T. Bosanquet. 2. Richard Nyren – he was in fact a left-hander. 3. South Africa v England at Cape Town in March 1892. Alec and G. G. Hearne played for England and their brother Frank for South Africa. 4. Both had previously played for Australia against England. 5. Ten days. It was left drawn. 6. All took a wicket with their first ball in Test cricket. 7. W. E. Midwinter. 8. Len Hutton. 9. Brian Close when he played against New Zealand at Manchester in 1949. He was 18 years 149 days. 10. W. R. Endean.

53. 1. Headingley, Leeds. 2. Shafiq Ahmed. 3. Majid Khan 75 runs. 4. Derek Underwood. 5. Alan Knott. 6. (a) Lord's (b) The Oval. 7. Zaheer Abbas. 8. Chris Old.

54. A. (a) Derbyshire (b) Chocolate, amber and pale blue (c) Rose and crown. B. (a) Middlesex (b) Blue (c) Three Seaxes. C. (a) Somerset (b) Black, white and maroon (c) Wessex Wyvern.

55. (a) Two players in each side were born in the county. Kitchen and Burgess of Somerset, and Brain and Yardley of Worcestershire. (b) Seven of Somerset – Taylor (Bucks), Close (Yorks), Parks (Sussex), Botham

(Cheshire), Breakwell (Staffs), Langford (Warwickshire) and Jones (Surrey). Four of Worcestershire – Ormrod and Gifford (both Lancs), Wilcock (Surrey) and Inchmore (Northumberland). (c) Two of Somerset – Richards and Moseley (both West Indies). Five of Worcestershire – Headley and Holder (both West Indies), Turner and Parker (both New Zealand) and D'Oliveira (South Africa).

56. A. There were only *two* stumps to a wicket when the game was played in 1775 so Stevens could not have knocked out John Small's middle stump. As a matter of fact an account of the match records that three times the ball passed through the two-stump wicket without disturbing the bail. Such incidents increased the feeling that three stumps should be used and from around 1776 a third was introduced. B. The Mound Stand at Lord's was not built until 1899. C. Until 1910, six runs were only scored from a single stroke (unless they were all run of course) if the ball went out of the ground. Otherwise a shot simply clearing the boundary, like the one fictionally described in the extract, would only have scored four runs in 1902.

57. 1. Yorkshire. 2. Nottinghamshire. 3. Kent at Tunbridge Wells. 4. Surrey. 5. Sussex at Eastbourne. 6. Leicestershire at Leicester. 7. Lancashire. 8. Glamorgan at Cardiff. 9. Middlesex. 10. Warwickshire. 11. Cambridge University. 12. Oxford University.

58. Harold Larwood.

59. 1. K. W. R. Fletcher. 2. D. C. S. Compton. 3. E. J. O. Hemsley. 4. P. B. H. May. 5. A. C. D. Ingleby-Mackenzie. 6. R. M. C. Gilliat. 7. G. R. J. Roope. 8. M. J. K. Smith.

60. If the first wicket fell without a run having been scored then No. 1 batsman (Hamilton) must have been out for a duck. Then Garwood (No. 2) and Hopkins (No. 3) took the score to 22 before the next wicket fell. We cannot be sure whether this was the wicket of Garwood or Hopkins but, after Talbot (No. 4) has come in, the third wicket falls without addition to the score of 22. Since Talbot was not dismissed without scoring, the second and third batsmen out must have been Garwood and Hopkins – it does not matter in which order since we know that between them they scored 22 runs. (You will notice that no extras were conceded during the innings). Garwood scored ten runs, therefore Hopkins must have scored 22 less 10 runs – 12 in fact. Now that we can insert the scores of Hamilton and Hopkins (0 and 12 respectively), we need only add the total of runs scored by them and the eight batsmen whose scores are printed (this comes to 118 runs) and to subtract this from the total number of runs scored (184) to determine Penn's score (66 runs).

61. 1. 1,981 for 35 wickets in the drawn match between South Africa and England at Durban in 1939. 2. 903 for 7 dec. by England against Australia at the Oval in 1938. 3. 234 in the match between Australia (153) and South Africa (36 and 35) 1931–32. 4. In 1938 at the Oval England beat Australia by an innings and 579 runs. 5. Five – for Australia against the West Indies at Kingston 1954–55. The batsmen were C. C. McDonald 127, R. N. Harvey 204, K. R. Miller 109, R. G. Archer 128 and R. Benaud 121. 6. 758 for 8 dec. in the same match. 7. 790 for 3 dec. against Pakistan at Kingston 1957–58. 8. Gary Sobers – 365 not out. 9. Len Hutton's 364 made in the match at the Oval already noted in the answers to (2) and (4) above. 10. Hanif Mohammad batted for 16 hours 39 minutes for Pakistan against the West Indies. He scored 337.

62. There is probably more than one way in which the bowler can get his wicket. Here is one of them – done in eleven balls. 1 – BOWLED 2 – BOILED 3 – BAILED 4 – WAILED 5 – WALLED 6 – WALKED 7 – TALKED 8 – TACKED 9 – TICKED 10 – TICKET 11 – Not required 12 – WICKET.

63. 1. Amiss 152 and Luckhurst 116. 2. Tony Greig. 3. Colin Cowdrey. 4. Tony Greig 110 in England's first innings in the First Test at Brisbane. 5. Walker who took 4 for 73. 6. Jeff Thomson. 7. Derek Underwood 30 runs. 8. Greg Chappell's seven catches was the record. His grandfather, who once took six catches, was Victor Richardson. 9. (a) Knott 51 runs (b) Titmus 61. 10. John Edrich was the new captain. In the Oval Test against Australia in 1972 he had briefly captained England when captain Ray Illingworth was off the field with a knee injury. 11. In the Fourth Test when their victory made them three-up with only two more Test matches to be played in the series. 12. Andy Roberts the Hampshire fast bowler. 13. Knott 106 not out in England's second innings. 14 (a) Melbourne (b) Peter Lever (c) Mike Denness.

64. 1. Bob Willis born Co. Durham, played Warwickshire. 2. Norman McVicker – Lancashire/Leicestershire. 3. John Snow – Worcestershire/Sussex. 4. David Bairstow – Yorkshire/Yorkshire. 5. Stewart Storey – Sussex/Surrey. 6. John Edrich – Norfolk/Surrey. 7. David Lloyd – Lancashire/Lancashire. 8. Ray Illingworth – Yorkshire/Leicestershire. 9. Jim Parks – Sussex/Somerset. 10. John Dye – Kent/Northamptonshire.

65. Final championship positions:

1.	Lancs.	13 pts.	68.42%
2.	Surrey	13	61.90
3.	Essex	5	55.55
4.	Yorks	8	44.44
5.	Glos.	2	16.16
6.	Sussex	−1	− 9.99
7.	M'sex	−1	−14.28
8.	Warwk	−1	−14.28
9.	Hants	−3	−27.27
10.	Notts	−3	−42.85
11.	Som.	−6	−50.00
12.	Kent	−8	−66.86
13.	Leics.	−9	−81.81
14.	Derby	−9	−100.00